W9-BMX-894

the
stocked
kitchen™

The Stocked Kitchen™ Creators

If you are in desperate need of kitchen organization and/or meal planning assistance, look no further. The Stocked Kitchen™ system allows you to cook great meals while reducing grocery bills, stress, and food waste.

Creators Sarah Kallio and Stacey Krastins are your guides to getting and staying "Stocked." They have invented The Stocked Kitchen™ concept to make cooking meals and entertaining easier. Sarah and Stacey have similar backgrounds, but polar opposite personalities. They are an "odd-couple", who have created a system that works effectively for both of them.

Sarah, a wife and mother of two, gorgeous girls, is a tenacious redhead who loves to laugh. Although she is sometimes a bit scattered ("Bzzbbppt!"), she is filled with creativity and passion.

Stacey, a wife and mother of two, handsome boys, is straight haired and straight talking. She is a determined, organized, perfectionist with a generous heart.

Together they have successfully launched The Stocked Kitchen™ concept through their books and website, and are co-owners of Stock, LLC.

Testimonials

"I love to cook, but I especially love to entertain. The hardest thing for me is putting together a menu and finding all of the ingredients at the grocery store. Plus, it always seems like I forget a vital ingredient, and I realize it after I have started cooking. Having a "Stocked" pantry makes entertaining easy and stress free!"

Andrea - Saginaw, MI

"I have two words for The Stocked Kitchen™...THANK YOU! As a busy mom working part-time with 15-month-old twins, I don't have time to think about prepping meals for get-togethers. As a result, I haven't had family or friends over for a meal in more than a year! Finally, there is a solution for people like me. I no longer have to spend time finding recipes and getting all the ingredients because I have it all at home ready to go thanks to The Stocked Kitchen™!"

Cheryl - Spring Lake, MI

"Before trying this, I was not comfortable in the kitchen, nor did I enjoy cooking, much less entertaining. I'm not sure how to best describe it, but using this concept gave me confidence and comfort with cooking. The Stocked Kitchen™ is NOT a recipe book; it is a system. It's the reverse of what you would typically do when meal planning. You start with the food you have and the system gives you multiple options on what to make, with no extra trips to the grocery store. Genius! Thank you Stacey and Sarah!"

Dawn - Grand Haven, MI

"I am not so much a foodie as a mom of three and full time attorney struggling to find time to hit the grocery store and put a nutritious dinner on the table every night. I am cynical. I'll admit it - law school does it to you. And the make and take, freeze and bake for 1 hour dishes I had already tried made my husband and kids even more skeptical. (They asked if this was going to be more "slop in a pan.") But your list has really streamlined my grocery shopping and your simple, family friendly recipes in straightforward formats are a hit. Thanks for making life easier."

Leslee - West Olive, MI

The Stocked Kitchen™

one grocery list...endless recipes

by

Sarah Kallio and Stacey Krastins

The Stocked Kitchen™. Copyright © 2009 Stock, LLC. All rights reserved. Printed in Muskegon, Michigan. No part of this book may be used or reproduced in any manner whatsoever without written permission except in the case of brief quotations embodied in critical articles and reviews. For information, contact Stock, LLC, 101 Washington, PMB 112, Grand Haven, Michigan 49417.

SECOND EDITION

This book was produced by
Stock, LLC
Sarah Kallio and Stacey Krastins, owners
101 Washington, PMB 112
Grand Haven, MI 49417
www.thestockedkitchen.com

Cover design by Stock, LLC
Book design by Stock, LLC
Photographs by Sue Beecham Photography, LLC
Some photography courtesy of Stock.Xchng®
Edited by Stock, LLC and Kristin Schutte
Printed by Custom Service Printers, Inc., Muskegon, Michigan

To Craig, Andrew, Charlie,

Larry, Lexie, and Ella -

thank you for all your unwavering love and support.

-S.K.s

Contents

The System

Start With the List!

We've all had that moment during the day when we ask with a pit in our stomach, "What am I going to make for dinner?" We stand in our kitchens having a conversation with ourselves, hopefully silently. "I don't have anything to make." "What I planned for doesn't sound good." "I don't have any time to cook let alone get to the store."

We are all searching for a way to make the process easier. Many of us get discouraged into pre-packaged complacency, which doesn't satisfy any real cravings. (We've never heard anyone say, "You know what sounds good? Powdered milk with dehydrated broccoli!") Book stores contain a myriad of cookbooks toting catch phrases like "Quick and Simple" or "Cheap and Easy." The recipes may be quick, but they often require us to purchase random ingredients which we need a pinch of and then will never use again. We have, in the past, cluttered our pantries, refrigerators, and cupboards with hundreds of dollars of cookbooks and specialty items like "red pepper paste." We were still left missing an easy to use, versatile, and effective system for getting dinner on the table. This is why we created The Stocked Kitchen™!

The Stocked Kitchen™ is the first complete meal creation system with only one standard list of groceries. If your kitchen is "Stocked" with these ingredients you will always have what you need to create any of our recipes. These recipes have been used for all our own dining needs, including meals for drop in guests, special occasions, and every night dinners for our families. This system encompasses all parts of the meal creation process from shopping, to storing, to cooking, to serving. The results are delicious, and "guest worthy" meals made from real, basic ingredients. We have proven The Stocked Kitchen™ system works. It has reduced our grocery bills, our stress levels, our trips to the market, and food waste. We create more delicious meals while removing the "handcuffs" of pre-planning. It is so simple..."Start with the list"...but once you've incorporated it into your life you will see how powerful The Stocked Kitchen™ philosophy can be. One grocery list, endless recipes!

2

How It All Started.

Looking back, we can't believe what two women and a Mac can do.

A third birthday party actually brought us together. Stacey's son Andrew invited Sarah's daughter Lexie to his big day. We met, connected, and began to meet for play-dates. While sitting and chatting, we soon realized that we have more in common with each other than just our children's ages. We both have engineering degrees and marketing experience, and have always desired to start our own businesses. (You could say we had entrepreneurial spirits in us that were struggling to come out.) In addition, we loved to cook and entertain. We both often found ourselves offering or being asked to host and organize bridal showers, baby showers, holiday parties, and reunions for family and friends. We were the only people we knew that had guests over regularly (up to 50 people in the backyard on a random Friday night). Friends and family would make comments like "How do you do it?" We decided to collaborate on an entertaining book to make it easier for everyone.

We wanted this book to be something that we ourselves could and would use in our own kitchens. We began by questioning why entertaining is so much work and so expensive? Over countless play-dates, we started to realize that what made hosting people costly and time consuming was the fact that most recipes called for random ingredients which required extra cost and trips to the market. To alleviate some of the work on us, we would often ask our husbands to pick up missing ingredients on their way home from work. They were even more confused than we were on where to find items like Tahini Paste. So, for our entertaining book, we decided to list all of the specialty items, explain where they could be found, and describe what they looked like. We also decided to limit each dinner party to only three specialty items...hmmm...actually, no, how about only one item?

"WAIT! WHY DO WE NEED ANY SPECIALTY ITEMS AT ALL?"

In fact, we already owned too many ingredients that didn't get used enough and didn't work together. We decided that what we needed was to invent a way to standardize the items of our kitchens without limiting our ability to create a wide variety of dishes.

Plus, we realized that this wasn't just important for entertaining, but this system could be incredibly beneficial for cooking in general!

We investigated our own pantries and asked ourselves what items could be used in multiple ways, what more common items could be used to substitute out specialty items, and more obviously, what items don't we ever use? We researched what would be found in traditional, ethnic pantries, and how to derive those flavors from ingredients that we already used. We then began to create recipes only using these ingredients to prove the system worked. After a year of ingredient negotiation and recipe development, we created The Stocked Kitchen™ Grocery List. This list is now the only list we use to make all our meals.

We had a list and a lot of recipes, and were in awe of what we had created. We couldn't wait to share it with all of our friends and family because we believed that they could benefit so much from the list and recipes. We did know, however, that we needed to protect our idea properly, so we contacted a lawyer and discussed our options with him. He was impressed by our concept and suggested we move forward with a Utility Patent for the "System And Method For Reducing Inventory Of Household Ingredients And Utensils." We also copyrighted the list and trademarked our brand name "The Stocked Kitchen™."

We then were able to begin to share The Stocked Kitchen™ philosophy and get people's opinions. We wrote and developed a prototype book called "Taste" and in just seven months, sold 900 copies, mostly in our small community through home shows, our website, and local retail stores. The world should never underestimate a woman's, let alone two mother's, ability to find creative and realistic solutions to a problem.

The Stocked Kitchen™ system is so integrated into our lives and has made cooking so much easier that it's hard to remember how we did it before. Since we've limited the ingredients that we use, we feel like we have so many more options. There is no more Sunday evening recipe planning sessions and grocery list making. There is no more standing in front of an open pantry, full of random ingredients, saying, "I have nothing to make." There is no more pre-packaged Lasagnas taking up room in our freezers for

4

"just in case." In fact, the most "planning" we do for meals is defrosting some meat and then choosing a recipe to cook it with, late in the afternoon. This system allows us to make dinners that are always "guest worthy" with little or no pre-planning, lower our grocery bills, and a waste a lot less food.

Dinner doesn't have to be an overwhelming task that you perform just to feed your family. In fact, we consider our most important guests are our husbands and children. We want to make them a meal that is healthy, cost effective, and delicious. We are also determined to be able to serve them options with less processed and prepackaged foods. Because the Grocery List is made up of mostly "real" foods, we have the option of making recipes with fewer additives. For the same reasons, it is easy to adapt this system into any dietary preference or need because all the ingredients can be purchased low fat, sugar free, organic, etc. Our concept of convenience is adopting a system that works, not just filling our homes with "convenience foods."

This business began with a 6-month-old, 20-month-old, and two 3-year-olds in tow. We've developed this business through the loss of jobs, the stress of creating a solid partnership, and potty training. We realize that we could have only traveled this journey together. We are two women who took their creative edge and honed problem solving skills, followed their dream, and created a business and a future, The Stocked Kitchen™.

5

Using the System
Get Stocked!

We've provided you with our story, now...let's get you "Stocked"! In this section we will share with you our suggestions for making your kitchen more organized, efficient, and "Stocked" with the ingredients on our list!

1) **Check out the Grocery List** – This list, being only slightly melodramatic, will utterly and completely change your life. We have included a magnetic pad, found in the back cover of this book, which is divided into sections based on grocery store layouts. The items within each of these sections are listed in alphabetical order. Although every grocery store is slightly different, the list is set up to flow with most markets' layouts. The magnetic back allows you to hang the list on your refrigerators and check off items as you need them. When you prepare for a shopping trip, just quickly check to see what you are missing from the list. There are plenty of spots to add other items that you need to pick up at the store: cereal, string cheese, and toilet paper. Also, see the ingredient Glossary found at the back of this book. This guide provides useful specifics on how to buy, use, and store the items on this list. You might look at it initially and think, "Oh my gosh, do I really have to go and buy all this stuff?" We believe that most of you have or have had recently about 80% of these items already in your kitchen. Start going through the list and start pulling out the items that you already have. Feel better?

2) **Purge** – Take the Grocery List and a pen and work on one section of the list at a time. Start going through your pantry, refrigerator, and freezer. Our very basic and absolute rule of thumb is if you haven't opened or used something in over a year and it's not on the list...get rid of it. Either toss it or give the non-perishable items to charity. Next, make a decision. Are you taking a leap of faith and becoming "Stocked" or are you going to just test the waters. In other words, are you willing to get rid of those packets of taco seasoning and broccoli rice, or are you going to use them up first? If you want to use them up first, that's fine. Come back and see us

using the system

6

when your cupboards are bare. If you enjoy the idea of living on the edge and are willing to give yourself to us body and soul...welcome...and again, toss or donate!

3) Clean, Organize, and Prep - No matter how tidy or untidy you are...and we know because we run the gamut in this category...take the time, while items are removed from your cupboards, refrigerators and freezers, to tidy up. Remove the crud, like coffee grounds or garlic clove skins, from your shelves and wash those produce drawers in your refrigerator.

Here are some of our suggestions for kitchen organizing.

✓ Store flour and sugars in canisters on your countertop. This makes them much more accessible, which is particularly helpful when you only need a small amount.

✓ If possible store your jelly roll pans (a.k.a. cookie sheets) and cooling racks vertically. This aids so much in getting to them quickly.

> **THE WASTE FACTOR:**
> There will probably be moments during this process that you feel like you are being wasteful. Stop, take a deep breath and ask yourself if the item that you are considering getting rid of has given you the return on investment that you had hoped for. You can't do anything about wasting money in the past. What you can do is begin to build a kitchen full of ingredients that work together and provide great results now.

✓ Keep like can goods together in your pantry. Stack all of your tomatoes (diced, paste, and sauce) in one area, and your canned beans in another. It will be much easier to find what you looking for and to determine when you need more.

✓ We try to keep like tools together, separating our baking and cooking utensils. We store measuring cups and spoons, spatulas, and whisks in one drawer and slotted spoons, turners, and tongs in another.

4) The Initial Shopping Trip - Now that you've cleared the clutter, the fun begins. We make check marks, on the Grocery List, next to all of the items that we are missing. This is all the pre-shopping planning we ever do.

We would suggest in this first shopping trip that you buy the canned goods in quantities of between 4 and 6. This should cover any of the recipes in the book. (Go to page 13 to see an additional list of items that we tend to buy in larger quantities.)

We wish we had had this book when we were setting up our first homes because our kitchens would have been "Stocked" the right way the first time. We now do it better...not because we are outstanding chefs, not because we have all the time in the world, but because we have an aid...we are simply, always prepared.

"HONEY, CAN YOU PICK THIS UP ON THE WAY HOME?"

In the past I think our poor husbands thought that we would send them into the grocery "Jungle" on a quest for the most obscure items imaginable just to test their innate hunting skills. I remember running into a male colleague at the market who looked utterly forlorn. As he stared up at the pastas, I said, "Need some help?" With a bit of desperation he said, "Where are the Ramen Noodles?" I told him that they were by the soups. With total dismay and sarcasm, he said, "Of course...because why would they be by the NOODLES?!?" For all husbands everywhere, The Stocked Kitchen™ is our gift to you. The List doesn't change. Once you've got it... you've got it!

8

Trust the List!

Part of this process is really just a leap of faith. You have to trust the fact that when you have these items in your house, you can always make something. That is our promise to you. By shopping this way you will always be prepared, you will save money, and you will throw out a lot less spoiled food. The one thing you have to do is believe...try not to revert back to old habits like frozen pizzas. Believe in the new found possibilities of your kitchen.

About three years ago we took the plunge. We did exactly what we suggested you do: purged, organized, and shopped "Stocked"! Since then, we've tested the list in the real world and worked hard to perfect it. This single grocery list has taken us through birthday parties, holidays, cocktail parties, and every night dinners with great success and a barrage of compliments.

The reason the list works is because we created it with a very clear objectives. This single Grocery List:

✓ can be used for every grocery shopping trip.

✓ is made up mostly of "real food" and limits the use of prepackaged, highly processed items.

✓ can be purchased for varying dietary needs or preferences: low-sodium, low-fat, organic, etc.

✓ is made up of many ingredients that can be stored for at least a few weeks without spoiling.

✓ is made up of ingredients that, when combined creatively, can produce exceptional and diverse dishes.

CRUSTY, LITTLE SOLDIERS
A huge benefit for us has been being able to get rid of all of those half-used bottles of salad dressings, cocktail sauce, tartar sauce, etc. We joke that they used to stand at attention along the bottom of our refrigerator door like crusty, little soldiers. We now make our own salad dressings as needed, and we no longer need to throw away so many half-used containers. Good for the environment and good for our pocket books!

Never Make a Wasted Trip!

Another great result of The Stocked Kitchen™ is now we shop smart. Although grocery shopping doesn't necessarily sound like a spree at Saks, we promise that by using this system, it just got a whole lot easier. We have small children and live in Michigan next to a big, beautiful lake that dumps snow on us unrelentingly in the winter. We don't have the time, desire, or energy to bundle up our little ones and make trips to the market for essentials like milk, let alone something called "champagne extract!" We want to use our time as effectively as possible when we are able to get to the market. Here are some of our suggestions for staying "Stocked."

✓ Always check for sales, but especially on the more expensive items. Whether we are out or not, we always check to see if frozen Shrimp, canned lump Crab Meat and the others meats on the list are on sale. We bring them home and, where appropriate, put them right in the freezer.

✓ If possible, buy canned goods by the case. They stay good, basically, forever. If you have the room to store them, it's much more economical to buy them in bulk. We love our warehouse retail chains for this!

✓ We recommend buying ingredients in the sizes suggested on the list. We have paid close attention, making sure sizes are usable and the least wasteful. We've erred on opening more cans than having half of the cans' contents go to waste.

✓ You don't always have to have every item on the list in stock. For instance, Vanilla Ice Cream is only used for dessert recipes. If you are not a dessert person, you don't always have to have this on hand. Obviously, Gorgonzola, Bleu, and Feta cheeses have unique flavors that may not be your cup of tea. If this is the case, don't buy them. Although it will certainly change the taste of your recipes (Isn't that the point?), equal amounts of Parmesan and Mozzarella can be generally substituted.

✓ Fresh Basil, Green Onions, and the Cabbage and Carrot Mix are probably the most volatile items when it comes to staying fresh. Basil is an excellent herb to keep growing in your kitchen, allowing you the best opportunity to always have it available. Often times your grocer will have fresh basil plants for sale. For all of these items, however, if you find that you are not using them enough, only buy them every other or every third grocery store trip.

✓ Spices are best if used within a year. When we purchase them, we use a permanent marker and write the date on them. Because we've limited the number of spices you need, it is a lot easier to use them up within the year! Also, we purchase the Chili Powder, Dried Minced Onions, Cinnamon, Italian Seasonings, Herbes de Provence, and Cumin in large containers to save money. We use them in so many of our recipes that we find ourselves able to use them up.

You will begin to see opportunities to stay "Stocked" everywhere. When we are on vacation, we look in specialty shops for gourmet Dijon Mustards, Maple Syrups, or Raspberry Jams or Jellies, instead of the purposeless items we purchased in the past. Buying "Stocked" is a luxury because you get the value out of the products you are investing in.

Use What You Have!

It was very important to us while we were writing our recipe section to not separate the recipes into Main Dish or Side sections. We wanted to focus on the ingredients themselves. We feel that this is the best way to begin to learn to cook with what you have. We now base our meals according to what is available, and not on a arbitrary recipe. If Chicken sounds good for dinner, we choose a recipe from our "Chicken" section. If we have a bag of potatoes that are starting to root, we choose a Potato dish. If no meat is thawed for dinner, we look in the Bean section for our Kidney Bean Tortilla Lasagna. It is almost impossible to do this with other cookbooks because most of the time you won't have all of the rest of the ingredients necessary to make that recipe.

By shopping with The Stocked Kitchen™ Grocery List you will only shop for what you need, and in reality, there are going to be days that you are less "Stocked" than others. Don't assume that just because you haven't shopped for awhile that you have nothing to make. We tend to only shop every 7 to 10 days and can always still pull a dinner together. We usually start by looking through the freezer for a meat to defrost. We also will try to find a use for an ingredient that might be on its way to spoiling. For both these reasons we have set up an Ingredient Index in the back of this book. The index lists every recipe page on which each ingredient on our Grocery List is found, except for Salt and Pepper. Again, this book allows you to effectively look up a recipe by ingredient because you are generally "Stocked" with the other ingredients needed.

You may find yourself becoming comfortable enough with the ingredients that you start to cook without a recipe. We have found that by only using the ingredients on the list, we know what they taste like and how they pair with other flavors. You may even be able to begin substituting "Stocked" ingredients for ingredients in your favorite recipes. This is a wonderful result of The Stocked Kitchen™ system and will help you to continue to add new recipes to your repertoire.

"Stock" Support

We have received phone calls from friends saying, "Do you offer tech support?" They have also said they wish we could be there with them while they cook. Although that isn't always possible, we have included tips and suggestions throughout the book that we use and trust. We want you to find this system to be realistic and helpful!

Whenever you see Sarah's head, she will be providing a cooking suggestion. Sarah loves to cook and problem solve. Her motto: "I vill find a way!" She has discovered some handy tips along this journey and is excited to share them with you!

Whenever you see Stacey's head, she will be providing a serving suggestion. Stacey loves to entertain and set a beautiful table. Her strengths are in organization and presentation. She has great ideas that will make your guests feel welcomed and impressed!

You may, also, begin to notice a SK next to the title of some of our recipes. These are The Stocked Kitchen™ signature dishes. Although we love all of our recipes, these are some of our favorites.

Within our recipes, we have capitalized any items found on our Grocery List, including Aluminum Foil, etc. This is our way to reemphasize to you that you are only using ingredients found on the Grocery List.

Below is a list of items that we buy in large quantities. We recommend purchasing canned goods by the case and some spices in the largest sizes available at our warehouse retail chains. You should determine how much you buy by your taste preferences, but the ingredients below are a great place to start.

beans	broth	cheddar cheese	chicken breasts
chili powder	cinnamon	corn	cumin
diced tomatoes	dried minced onions	garlic powder	herbes de provence
italian seasoning	mozzarella cheese	nuts	oils
pasta	rice	sugar	tomato sauce

We have included this chart to clarify the symbols we use throughout this book.

C	Cup
T	Tablespoon
t	teaspoon
oz.	ounce
pkg.	package
lb.	pound

Cup (C)	=	Fluid OZ (oz.)	=	Tablespoon (T)	=	Teaspoon (t)
1 C		8 oz		16 T		48 t
3/4 C		6 oz		12 T		36 t
2/3 C		5 1/3 oz		10.6 T		32 t
1/3 C		4 oz		5.3 T		16 t
1/4 C		2 2/3 oz		4 T		12 t
1/8 C		1 oz		2 T		6 t
1/16 C		1/2 oz		1 T		3 t

This chart aids with equivalents.

14

A "Stocked" Week in Review.

On the next two pages is an example of an average week for us, using The Stocked Kitchen™ system. We all have busy schedules; however, the time frame that we have to make dinner varies from night to night. The Stocked Kitchen™ system is flexible enough to be realistic for our lives.

Sunday - Soups and Bread Bowls or Flank Steak Roll-Ups with Mashed Potatoes

Our hearty soups are perfect for a day when we have time to let them simmer for awhile, and they are especially great for Game Days! Some Sundays, however, we have the family over for a more formal meal. Flank Steak Roll-Ups are our answer to the roast!

Monday - Chicken Rice or Pasta Bake

On Monday we have the time to let something bake in the oven but not the energy after a busy weekend to be in the kitchen for a long time preparing it. Our baked chicken or pasta dishes are ideal for this.

Tuesday - Salad and Topper

Between our husbands' volleyball and golf leagues, they generally want something fast and light. One of our salad recipes topped with a grilled chicken breast or flank steak is perfect for these nights.

Wednesday - Pasta or Rice

We make one of the pasta or rice recipes a complete meal by adding the suggested meat toppings. If we have time, we add a vegetable side dish or salad. If we have thought ahead, we add some fresh baked bread.

Thursday Night - Fast Food or Leftovers

With our children's' dance classes and soccer practice, Thursday nights seem to be our busiest. When we say "fast food," we don't mean drive-through. Here are some ideas for great food fast.

✓ Pancakes and Sausage
✓ Grilled Ham and Cheese Sandwiches
✓ Chef Salads with ranch dressing
✓ Pita Pizzas
✓ Sloppy Joes
✓ Taco Meat and Taco Salads

Friday Night - Cocktails and Appetizers With Friends

Many of our appetizers are hearty enough to act as mini meals. Add some cocktails, and you have a perfect night in with friends!

Saturday Night

This is our free-for-all night. It might be leftovers; we might get a babysitter and go out to dinner (PB&J for the kids), or we might make a Homemade Pizza. Saturday nights are our wild card.

You are now "Stocked" and ready. It is time to put the system to the test. Our hope for you is that you will experience the same benefits with this system that we have. We wish you more manageable grocery bills, effortless meal planning, and delicious recipes. The only question now is...what do you make first?

The List

The only items you need to make any of the recipes in this book!

the stocked kitchen™ grocery list

pantry	spices	freezer
applesauce	anise seed/fennel seed	bread dough
apricot preserves	chili powder	broccoli
artichoke hearts, marinated	cinnamon, ground	green beans
barbecue sauce	cumin, ground	peas
beans, black (15 oz.)*	dill weed	puff pastry sheets
beans, kidney (15 oz.)*	garlic powder	shrimp (raw, peeled, de-veined)
beans, northern/cannelini (15 oz.)*	grill seasoning	spinach (bag)
broth, beef (15 oz.)*	herbes de provence	vanilla ice cream
broth, chicken (15 oz.)*	italian seasoning	
bread crumbs, plain	nutmeg, whole/ground	
coffee, regular and decaf	onions, dried minced	**meat, chicken, and seafood**
corn (15 oz.)*	peppercorns/pepper	bacon
honey	poultry seasoning	chicken breast (boneless, skinless)
horseradish, prepared	pumpkin pie spice	chicken thighs (boneless, skinless)
ketchup	red pepper flakes	crab meat, imitation/canned lump
mandarin oranges (10 oz.)*	salt	flank steak/flat iron steak
maple syrup	**baking**	ground beef/turkey/chicken
mayonnaise	baking powder	ground breakfast sausage
mushrooms (4 oz.)*	baking soda	ham, slice/whole
mustard, dijon	brownie mix (8x8 inch)*	
mustard, yellow	cake mix, yellow	
olives, black (4 oz.)*	chocolate chips, semi-sweet	**produce**
olives, green/calamata	chocolate chips, white	apples
pancake mix	cocoa powder	basil, fresh
peanut butter, creamy	extract, almond	bell pepper, red/green
pears (15 oz.)*	extract, peppermint	cabbage and carrot mix
pineapple, slices/chunks (15 oz.)*	extract, vanilla	carrots
raspberry jam/jelly	flour, all-purpose	celery
ranch/buttermilk dressing	food coloring	cranberries, dried
relish, sweet/dill	non-stick spray	cucumber, english
tabasco/hot sauce	nuts, almonds	garlic
tomatoes, diced (15 oz.)*	nuts, peanuts	ginger (tube/jar)
tomato paste (4 oz. can/tube)*	nuts, pecans	green onions
tomato sauce (15 oz.)*	oil, extra virgin olive	lemons
vinegar, aged balsamic	oil, vegetable	lemon juice
vinegar, red wine	sugar, brown	lettuce, head/mixed greens
vinegar, white wine	sugar, granulated	limes/lime juice
worcestershire sauce	sugar, powdered	pine nuts
	refrigerated	potatoes, russet/sweet/yukon gold
international	butter, unsalted	raisins
egg noodles	cheese, bleu/gorgonzola	shallots/onion
pasta, penne/fusilli/farfalle	cheese, cheddar	tomatoes
pasta, thin	cheese, feta	
rice, jasmine/brown	cheese, mozzarella (shredded)	
roasted red peppers	cheese, parmesan	**other supplies**
salsa	cream cheese	aluminum foil
soy sauce	cream, heavy/whipping	parchment paper
snacks, crackers, and bread	eggs	plastic wrap
bread loaf, white/wheat	milk	skewers, wooden
butter crackers	sour cream/plain yogurt	storage bags, resealable gallon
pita bread	tortillas, flour (8"/fajita size)	toothpicks
tortilla chips		

www.thestockedkitchen.com

* approximate sizes   Copyright 2009 Stock, LLC All Rights Reserved

Appetizers

BACON WRAPS
Bacon Wrapped Artichoke Hearts (p.19)
Bacon Wrapped Pineapple (p.20)
Bacon Wrapped Ranch Chicken (p.20)
Bacon Wrapped Shrimp (p.21)

BLENDED CHILLED DIPS & DIPPERS
Hummus (p.22)
Roasted Red Pepper Dip (p.22)
Sweet Pea Pesto Dip (p.23)
Garlic Toast (p.24)
Pita Chips (p.24)
Seasoned Pita Chips (p.25)

CHEESE BALLS
Bleu Cheese Cranberry Cheese Ball (p.26)
Caramel Apple Cheese Ball (p.26)
Pesto Cheese Ball (p.27)

COLD DIPS
Cajun Aioli (p.28)
Dill Dip (p.29)
Spinach Dip (p.29)

CREAM CHEESE LAYERED DIPS
Black Bean Layered Dip (p.30)
Crab Cocktail Layered Dip (p.30)
Olive Puree Layered Dip (p.31)
Pineapple Apricot Layered Dip (p.31)
Salsa Layered Dip (p.32)

DEVILED EGGS (p.33)

HOT DIPS
Hot Black Bean Dip (p.34)
Hot Crab Dip (p.35)
Hot Spinach Artichoke Dip (p.35)
Hot Stuffed Mushroom Dip (p.36)

LETTUCE WRAPS
Asian Lettuce Wraps (p.37)
Chophouse Lettuce Wraps (p.38)
Sweet and Tangy Lettuce Wraps (p.39)

PUFF PASTRY BITES
Antipasto Bites (p.40)
Crab Rangoons (p.41)
Egg Rolls with Sweet & Sour Sauce (p.42)
Empanadas with Cajun Aioli (p.43)
Ham and Cheese Bites (p.44)
Spinach and Feta Bites (p.44)

SALSAS
Black Bean Mandarin Orange Salsa (p.45)
Cucumber Thai Salsa (p.46)
Italian Salsa / Bruschetta (p.47)
Pineapple Tomato Salsa (p.48)

SAUSAGE MEATBALLS
Sausage Meatballs (p.49)
Barbecue Sauce (p.49)
Ginger Sauce (p.50)
Raspberry Sauce (p.50)
Teriyaki Sauce (p.51)

TORTILLA ROLL-UPS
Greek Tortilla Roll-Ups (p.52)
Ham and Relish Tortilla Roll-Ups (p.53)
Vegetable Tortilla Roll-Ups (p.54)

black bean layered dip

blended chilled dips

cucumber thai salsa

bacon wraps

puff pastry bites

vegetable tortilla roll-ups

BACON WRAPS

These quick, individual bites are dedicated to Sarah's husband Larry and his absolute love of Bacon! Enjoy these as appetizers or as delicious salad toppers!

Bacon Wrapped Artichoke Hearts

MAKES 30

- 5 slices Bacon
- 30 Marinated Artichoke Hearts, drained

1. Preheat oven to 425°F.   Line a jelly roll pan with Aluminum Foil and then top with a cooling rack.
2. Cut slices of Bacon into thirds and then cut the thirds in half lengthwise. Wrap Artichoke Hearts with pieces of Bacon and secure with Toothpicks.
3. Lay on top of jelly roll pan. Bake for 20 minutes or until Bacon is crispy.

BACON COOKING TIP

This is absolutely the easiest, cleanest, and least stinky way to cook bacon!

1. Preheat oven to 425°F.
2. Line a jelly roll pan with Aluminum Foil and then top with a cooling rack.
3. Lay bacon flat on cooling rack being careful not to overlap.
4. Bake for 20 minutes. Dab with paper towel to remove excess grease.

20

Bacon Wrapped Pineapple

MAKES 30

- 5 slices Bacon
- 30 Pineapple chunks, drained
- 1/4 C Brown Sugar

1. Preheat oven to 425°F. Line a jelly roll pan with Aluminum Foil and then top with a cooling rack.
2. Cut slices of Bacon into thirds and then cut the thirds in half lengthwise. Wrap Pineapple chunks with pieces of Bacon and secure with Toothpicks. Dip into Brown Sugar.
3. Lay on top of jelly roll pan. Bake for 20 minutes or until Bacon is crispy.

Bacon Wrapped Ranch Chicken

MAKES 24

- 4 slices Bacon
- 4 Boneless Skinless Chicken Breasts (or 6 Thighs), uncooked, cubed into 24 pieces
- 1/4 C Ranch Dressing
- 2 T Grill Seasoning

1. Preheat oven to 425°F. Line a jelly roll pan with Aluminum Foil and then top with a cooling rack.
2. Soak Chicken cubes in Ranch Dressing for a few minutes, making sure to completely submerge each piece. Drain Ranch Dressing and toss Chicken with Grill Seasoning.
3. Cut slices of Bacon into thirds and then cut the thirds in half lengthwise. Wrap Chicken chunks with pieces of Bacon and secure with Toothpicks.
4. Lay on top of jelly roll pan. Bake for 20 minutes or until Bacon is crispy.

Bacon Wrapped Shrimp SK

MAKES 30

- 5 slices Bacon
- 30 Shrimp, raw, peeled, de-tailed, and thawed
- 1/4 C Barbecue Sauce

1. Preheat oven to 425°F. Line a jelly roll pan with Aluminum Foil and then top with a cooling rack.
2. Cut slices of Bacon into thirds and then cut the thirds in half lengthwise. Wrap Shrimp with pieces of Bacon and secure with Toothpicks.
3. Lay on top of jelly roll pan and baste with Barbecue Sauce. Bake for 20 minutes or until Bacon is crispy.

BLENDED CHILLED DIPS AND DIPPERS

These dips are full of flavor and extremely fast and easy to make. We love them with the Pita Chips and Garlic Toast recipes on the following pages.

Hummus SK

SERVES 4

- 2 15 oz. can Northern/Cannelini Beans, drained and rinsed
- 1/3 C Warm Water
- 1/4 C Peanut Butter
- 1/4 C Lemon Juice
- 1/4 C Olive Oil
- 2 cloves Garlic, minced
- 1 t Cumin
- 1 t Salt

1. Add ingredients to a blender/food processor and pulse until smooth.
2. Chill and serve with Pita Chips or Garlic Toast.

Roasted Red Pepper Dip

SERVES 4

- 7 oz. jar Roasted Red Peppers, drained
- 1/4 C Fresh Basil, roughly chopped
- 1 T Balsamic Vinegar
- 2 T Olive Oil
- 1/2 C Feta Cheese

1. Add ingredients to a blender/food processor and pulse until smooth.
2. Chill and serve with Pita Chips or Garlic Toast.

Sweet Pea Pesto Dip

SERVES 4

- 2 C Frozen Peas, thawed and drained
- 2 cloves Garlic, minced
- 1/4 C Olive Oil

- 1/4 C Parmesan Cheese
- 1/4 C Fresh Basil, chopped
- 1/4 C Water

1. Add ingredients to a blender/food processor and pulse until smooth.
2. Chill and serve with Pita Chips or Garlic Toast.

DIFFERENT GUESTS - DIFFERENT TASTES
Everyone we have tested these dips on have really liked at least one of them. Because they are so simple to make and can be made ahead of time, we like to make all three dips when entertaining. They look beautiful displayed together and have enough variety of flavors that everyone will find at least one favorite! (See photo page at the front of this section.)

24

Garlic Toast

SERVES 4

- 6 slices Bread, crusts removed
- 2 T Unsalted Butter, melted
- 1/4 t Garlic Powder

1. Preheat oven to 400°F.
2. Mix Butter and Garlic Powder and brush over slices. Cut Bread slices into 4 triangles.
3. Bake on a Parchment Paper covered jelly roll pan for 12 minutes.

Pita Chips

SERVES 4

- 4 Pita Bread

1. Preheat oven to 400°F.
2. Cut Pitas into 8 triangles.
3. Bake on Parchment Paper covered jelly roll pan for 8 minutes.

PARCHMENT PAPER

Parchment paper topped jelly roll pans make these Dippers' clean-up effortless! Parchment paper makes pans truly non-stick. Do not confuse parchment paper with wax paper which can leave a wax residue when baking.

Seasoned Pita Chips

SERVES 4

- 4 Pita Bread
- 2 T Olive Oil
- 1/4 t Garlic Powder
- 1/2 t Salt

1. Preheat oven to 400°F.
2. Mix Garlic Powder and Salt. Brush Oil over Pita. Sprinkle with Salt mixture. Cut Pitas into 8 triangles.
3. Bake on Parchment Paper covered jelly roll pan for 8 minutes.

CHEESE BALLS
Cheese Balls are wonderful make-ahead appetizers.
Kids will LOVE the Caramel Apple!

Bleu Cheese Cranberry Cheese Ball

SERVES 8

- 1 8 oz. pkg. Cream Cheese, softened
- 1/2 C Dried Cranberries, chopped
- 1/2 C Cheddar Cheese, shredded
- 1/4 C Bleu/Gorgonzola Cheese
- 1/4 C Pecans, finely chopped

1. Mix Cream Cheese, Cranberries, and Cheeses together.
2. Place mixture in Aluminum Foil or Plastic Wrap and form into a ball. Refrigerate for at least 30 minutes.
3. Roll in chopped Pecans. Serve with Crackers and/or Celery Sticks.

Caramel Apple Cheese Ball SK

SERVES 8

- 1 8 oz. pkg. Cream Cheese, softened
- 2 T Peanut Butter
- 1/2 C Brown Sugar
- 1 t Vanilla
- 1/4 C Peanuts, chopped

1. Mix Cream Cheese, Peanut Butter, Brown Sugar, and Vanilla with an electric hand mixer.
2. Place mixture in Aluminum Foil or Plastic Wrap and form into a ball. Refrigerate for at least 30 minutes.
3. Roll in chopped Peanuts right before serving. Serve with Apple Slices tossed with Lemon or Lime Juice to prevent Apples from turning brown.

Pesto Cheese Ball

SERVES 8

- 2 C Fresh Basil, roughly chopped
- 3 T Pine Nuts
- 1/4 C Parmesan Cheese
- 2 cloves Garlic
- 1 T Olive Oil

- 1/4 t Black Pepper
- 1 8 oz. pkg. Cream Cheese, softened
- 1 C Mozzarella Cheese, shredded
- 1/2 C Roasted Red Pepper, well drained and finely chopped

1. In a blender or food processor, blend together Basil, Pine Nuts, Parmesan, Garlic, Olive Oil and Pepper until smooth.
2. Mix together with remaining ingredients. Place mixture in Aluminum Foil or Plastic Wrap and form into a ball. Refrigerate for at least 30 minutes.
3. Serve with Crackers, Pita Chips, or crudités.

HAVE DIP, WILL TRAVEL
For those times when we are asked to bring a dish to pass, we love these Cheese Balls because they travel well. We bring along a platter, and assemble the Cheese Ball and accompaniment when we arrive at our destination. The Pesto Cheese Ball in particular is a festive choice for the holidays because of its green and red coloring.

COLD DIPS

These are great dips to have in your back pocket. They are perfect with cut up vegetables, including Carrots, Celery, Bell Peppers, and Cucumbers.

Cajun Aioli SK

SERVES 6

- 1 C Mayonnaise
- 12 drops Tabasco/Hot Sauce
- 1/2 t Garlic Powder
- 1 T Chili Powder

- 1/2 T Dried Minced Onions
- 1/4 t Nutmeg
- 1/2 t Pepper

1. Mix ingredients together and chill.

RECIPES LISTED MULTIPLE TIMES

We have erred on the side of listing recipes more than once in this book. We prefer to have the accompanying recipe on the same page instead of having to flip through the book to find it.

Cajun Aioli is a great example of this. You will find it here, with the Empanadas, and as a condiment for the Southwest Burger. We actually love to serve this "dip" with cut up vegetables and Empanadas on the same platter. This provides your guests with more options without having to make another whole recipe!

Dill Dip

SERVES 6

- 1 C Mayonnaise
- 1 C Sour Cream/Plain Yogurt
- 1 T Minced Onions
- 1/2 t Herbes de Provence
- 1 T Dill Weed
- 1/4 t Salt

1. Mix ingredients together and chill for at least one hour.

Spinach Dip

SERVES 6

- 1 10 oz. pkg. Frozen Spinach, thawed and squeezed dry
- 1 C Sour Cream/Plain Yogurt
- 1 C Mayonnaise
- 2 T Dried Minced Onions
- 1/2 C Pine Nuts
- 1/4 t Garlic Powder
- 1/2 t Herbes de Provence
- 1 T Lemon Juice
- 1/4 t Pepper
- 1 t Salt

1. Blend ingredients together well and chill for at least one hour. Serve with vegetables or Pita Chips.

HOW TO DRAIN SPINACH
Frozen spinach retains an enormous amount of water when thawed and must be "squeezed dry." We like using a clean kitchen towel or sturdy paper towel to wrap around the spinach and squeeze out excess water. A small colander also works well so we can push the water out through the bottom.

CREAM CHEESE LAYERED DIPS

These Cream Cheese based, layered dips are simple and flavorful. They are a perfect as a meal starter or dish to pass.

Black Bean Layered Dip

SERVES 8

- 1 15 oz. can Black Beans, drained and rinsed
- 1 pkg. Cream Cheese, softened
- 1 C Salsa
- 1 C Lettuce, finely chopped (optional)

- 1 C Cheddar Cheese, shredded
- 3 Green Onions, chopped (optional)
- 1 4 oz. can Black Olives, sliced or diced (optional)

1. Mash Black Beans and mix together with Cream Cheese and Salsa until well blended.
2. Spread over bottom of pie plate. Layer with Lettuce, Cheese, Onions, and Olives.
3. Serve with Tortilla Chips.

Crab Cocktail Layered Dip SK

SERVES 8

- 1 pkg. Cream Cheese, softened
- 6 oz. pkg. Crab Meat, imitation (finely chopped) or canned lump (drained)

COCKTAIL SAUCE
- 1/2 C Ketchup
- 2 T Prepared Horseradish
- 1 T Lemon Juice

1. Spread Cream Cheese over the bottom of a pie plate.
2. Mix COCKTAIL SAUCE ingredients together, spread over Cream Cheese and sprinkle with Crab.
3. Chill and serve with Butter Crackers.

Olive Puree Layered Dip

SERVES 8

- 1 pkg. Cream Cheese, softened
- 1/4 C Almonds
- 2 T Lemon Juice
- 1 C Green/Calamata Olives
- 1 T Worcestershire Sauce
- 1/4 C Olive Oil
- 1 T Herbes de Provence
- 1/4 t Pepper

1. Spread Cream Cheese over the bottom of a pie plate.
2. In a food processor, add ingredients and pulse until a paste forms.
3. Spread over Cream Cheese and serve with Butter Crackers or Carrot sticks.

Pineapple Apricot Layered Dip

SERVES 8

- 1 pkg. Cream Cheese, softened
- 1/2 C Apricot Preserves
- 1/2 C Pineapple, drained and chopped
- 1 T Prepared Horseradish
- 1 T Dijon Mustard

1. Spread Cream Cheese over the bottom of a pie plate.
2. In a saucepan over medium heat, mix remaining ingredients and heat until mixture bubbles.
3. Pour over Cream Cheese and serve with Butter Crackers.

32

Salsa Layered Dip

SERVES 8

- 1 pkg. Cream Cheese, softened
- 1 C Salsa

1. Spread Cream Cheese over the bottom of a pie plate. Pour Salsa over top of Cream Cheese.
2. Either chill or heat in microwave for approximately 45 seconds. Serve with Tortilla Chips.

HOT OR COLD
This is a great appetizer all year round. In the summer we like to keep it cold, but in the winter we heat it up in the microwave and serve it warm. Either way it is delicious and about as simple as it gets!

Deviled Eggs are a great tradition for summer backyard BBQs, but these are anything but old-fashioned. Enjoy any season, any time!

Deviled Eggs

SERVES 12

- 12 Eggs
- 1/2 C Mayonnaise
- 1 T Dried Minced Onions
- 1 t Yellow Mustard

- 1/4 t Dill Weed
- 1/4 t Chili Powder
- 1/8 t Salt

1. Place Eggs in a stock pot and cover with water by at least an inch. Over high heat, bring water to a rolling boil. Remove from heat, cover, and allow to cook in the warm water (removed from burner) for 18 minutes. Drain water and cover with ice cubes or very cold tap water. Allow to sit for a few minutes, drain and refill with ice or cold tap water.
2. Peel Eggs and cut in half lengthwise. Remove yolks and combine with remaining ingredients. Scoop a teaspoon of mixture back into each Egg white half and serve.

PEELING EGGS

Hard-boiled eggs can be maddening to peel when the shell clings to the egg like it is its job. The above cooking method seems to help with this problem. We also tap both ends of the egg and then gently roll the side of the egg on our kitchen counters to create many little cracks in the shell before we peel!

HOT DIPS

These warm hearty dips are always a hit. To make them ahead of time, cover and place in refrigerator before baking and then bake just prior to serving.

Hot Black Bean Dip

SERVES 8

- 1 can Black Beans, rinsed and drained
- 1 T Cumin
- 1 T Chili Powder
- 1/2 t Salt
- 1/3 C Salsa
- 1/2 C Cheddar Cheese, shredded
- 1/4 C Green or Black Olives, chopped (optional)

1. Preheat oven to 400°F.
2. Mix together Beans, Cumin, Chili Powder, Salt, and Salsa.
3. Transfer to a pie plate or 8" square baking dish and top with Cheese and Olives.
4. Bake for 10 minutes. Serve with Tortilla Chips.

Hot Crab Dip

SERVES 8

- 8 oz. pkg. Cream Cheese
- 1/3 C Mayonnaise
- 2 t Lemon Juice
- 1 T Water
- 2 Green Onions, sliced
- 1 T Herbes de Provence

- 1 T Prepared Horseradish
- 1/4 t Worcestershire Sauce
- 8 drops Tabasco/Hot Sauce
- 1/2 C Almonds, chopped
- 1 6 oz. pkg. Crab Meat, imitation (chopped) or canned lump (drained)

1. Preheat oven to 400°F.
2. Mix all the ingredients together and spread out into a pie plate or 8" square baking dish.
3. Bake for 20 minutes. Serve with Butter Crackers.

Hot Spinach Artichoke Dip SK

SERVES 8

- 1 C Mayonnaise
- 1 15 oz. jar Marinated Artichoke Hearts, drained

- 1 C Frozen Spinach, thawed and squeezed dry
- 1 C Mozzarella Cheese
- 1/3 C Parmesan Cheese

1. Preheat oven to 400°F.
2. Mix all of the ingredients together and spread out into a pie plate or 8" square baking dish.
3. Bake for 20 minutes. Serve with Tortilla Chips or Pita Chips.

36

Hot Stuffed Mushroom Dip

SERVES 8

- 2 4 oz. cans Sliced Mushrooms, drained and chopped
- 1/2 C Mayonnaise
- 1 6 oz. pkg. Crab Meat, imitation (chopped) or canned lump (drained)
- 2 T Green Onions, sliced
- 1/4 C Milk
- 1 t Dijon Mustard
- 1/4 C Plain Bread Crumbs
- 1 t Herbs De Provence
- 1/2 C Mozzarella Cheese
- 1/4 C Parmesan Cheese

1. Preheat oven to 400°F.
2. Mix all the ingredients together and spread out into a pie plate or 8" square baking dish.
3. Bake for 20 minutes. Serve with Butter Crackers.

LETTUCE WRAPS

Lettuce Wraps make a great starter or main dish. Any of these mixtures are tasty wrapped in Tortillas, too!

Asian Lettuce Wraps

SERVES 4

- 1 lb. Ground Beef
- 1 4 oz. can Mushrooms
- 1/4 C Green Onion, sliced
- 1 C Cabbage and Carrot Mixture

- 1/4 t Garlic Powder
- 1/4 C Soy Sauce
- 1/4 C Brown Sugar
- 1 t White Wine Vinegar

1. In a fry pan, cook Ground Beef thoroughly and drain off grease.
2. Add Mushrooms, Green Onion, Cabbage and Carrot Mixture, and Garlic Powder. Saute over medium heat until vegetables begin to soften.
3. Mix together Soy Sauce, Brown Sugar and White Wine Vinegar. Pour over meat mixture and cook until heated through.
4. Serve with Lettuce leaves for wrapping.

LETTUCE FOR LETTUCE WRAPS

Our preference for Lettuce Wraps is either Iceberg, Boston, or Bibb lettuce. Iceberg is easily found and inexpensive. We cut the Iceberg head into quarters and serve.

Boston and Bibb are small and the leaves are already the perfect size for wrapping. Be sure to clean thoroughly before serving. (Don't mistake mini cabbages for these lettuces.) ☺

38

Chophouse Lettuce Wraps

SERVES 4

- 3 T Ketchup
- 3 T Worcestershire Sauce
- 1 T Maple Syrup
- 1 T Chili Powder
- 1 t Prepared Horseradish
- 1 T Unsalted Butter

- 1 Shallot or Onion, thinly sliced
- 1 lb. Flank Steak, sliced thin against the grain
- 1 4 oz. can Mushrooms, drained
- 1/2 C Bleu/Gorgonzola Cheese
- 1 T Grill Seasoning

1. Mix together Ketchup, Worcestershire Sauce, Maple Syrup, Chili Powder, and Horseradish and set aside.
2. In a fry pan over medium high heat, melt Butter. Add Onions and cook until they are softened. Add Steak and continue cooking until Steak is brown on the outside and pink on the inside.
3. Mix Mushrooms and Ketchup mixture with Steak and Onions. Toss entire mixture with Grill Seasoning.
4. Sprinkle with Bleu Cheese and serve with Lettuce leaves for wrapping.

Sweet and Tangy Lettuce Wraps

SERVES 4

- 12 oz. - 1 lb. Boneless Skinless Chicken (chopped into 1 inch pieces), or Shrimp, thawed and de-tailed.
- 2 T Vegetable Oil
- 1/2 t Garlic Powder
- 1 Bell Pepper, thinly sliced
- 3 Green Onions, thinly sliced
- 1 C Cabbage and Carrot Mixture
- 1/2 C Fresh Basil, finely chopped

GLAZE
- 1/4 C Applesauce
- 2 T Apricot Preserves
- 1/2 T Honey
- 1/4 C White Wine Vinegar
- 2 T Ginger
- 1 T Worcestershire Sauce
- 3 T Soy Sauce

1. Mix together GLAZE ingredients in a bowl and set aside.
2. In a fry pan over high heat, cook Chicken or Shrimp in Oil. Add Garlic Powder and Peppers, Onions, and Cabbage Mix, and cook for 2-3 minutes.
3. Pour GLAZE over Chicken/Shrimp and Vegetables, sprinkle with Basil, and toss to coat. Serve with Lettuce leaves for wrapping.

PUFF PASTRY BITES

These individual appetizers are all delicious and impressive. Add variety by using one mini muffin pan for two different recipes. Just make sure to cut the filling recipes in half.

Antipasto Bites SK

MAKES 24

- 1 sheet Puff Pastry, thawed
- 1/4 C Green/Calamata Olives, chopped
- 1/2 C Marinated Artichoke Hearts, chopped
- 1 Roasted Red Pepper, diced
- 1/2 C Mozzarella Cheese

1. Preheat oven to 400°F. Thaw a sheet of Puff Pastry and roll out on a floured surface to approximately 11"x14".
2. With a pizza cutter cut sheet into 24 pieces (4 rows & 6 columns). Stretch pastry squares slightly and lay into cups of a mini muffin pan.
3. Mix together Olives, Artichoke Hearts, and Roasted Red Pepper.
4. Fill cups with 1 teaspoon of the mix and then top with Mozzarella Cheese.
5. Bake for 12 - 15 minutes or until corners begin to brown.

USING PUFF PASTRY

Puff pastry may seem intimidating, however, it is really easy to use and very forgiving. To thaw, remove from wrapper and set out on counter. If thawing two sheets, be sure to separate and lay on counter side by side. It takes approx. 30 - 40 minutes to thaw. Puff pastry works best when it is still cold before baking. (This allows the fat to stay solid and melt while baking, causing little pockets of air, or what we taste as puffed flakiness.) If while working with the dough it has become warm, place in fridge while you mix the fillings.

Crab Rangoons

MAKES 24

- 1 sheet Puff Pastry, thawed
- 1 T Sour Cream
- 1/2 8 oz. pkg. Cream Cheese, softened
- 1/2 6 oz. pkg. Crab Meat, imitation (chopped) or canned lump (drained)
- 1 Green Onion, thinly sliced
- 1/8 t Garlic Powder
- 1 t Ginger
- 1 t Soy Sauce
- 2 T Powdered Sugar

1. Preheat oven to 400°F. Thaw a sheet of Puff Pastry and roll out on a floured surface to approximately 11"x14".
2. With a pizza cutter cut sheet into 24 pieces (4 rows & 6 columns). Stretch pastry squares slightly and lay into cups of a mini muffin pan.
3. Mix together remaining ingredients.
4. Fill cups with 1 teaspoon of the mixture.
5. Bake for 12 - 15 minutes or until corners begin to brown.

42

Egg Rolls with Sweet and Sour Sauce

MAKES 24

- 1 sheets Puff Pastry, thawed
- 1 T Vegetable Oil
- 1 T Ginger
- 1/2 t Garlic Powder
- 1 (4 oz. can) Mushrooms, drained

- 1 C Cabbage and Carrot Mix
- 1 Green Onions, finely chopped
- 1 T Soy Sauce
- 1/8 t Pepper
- 1 Egg, white only, lightly beaten

1. Preheat oven to 400°F. Thaw a sheet of Puff Pastry and roll out on a floured surface to approximately 11"x14".
2. With a pizza cutter cut sheet into 24 pieces (4 rows & 6 columns). Stretch pastry squares slightly and lay into cups of a mini muffin pan.
3. In fry pan, heat Oil over medium heat, mix in Ginger, Garlic Powder, Mushrooms, Cabbage Mixture, and Green Onions. Cook 2-3 minutes until vegetables soften.
4. Mix in Soy Sauce, Pepper, and Egg White until Egg is scrambled.
5. Fill each cup with 1 teaspoon of mixture.
6. Bake for 12 - 15 minutes or until corners begin to brown. Serve with Sweet and Sour Sauce below.

Sweet and Sour Sauce

- 3 T Apricot Preserves
- 2 T Ketchup
- 2 T Brown Sugar
- 2 T Soy Sauce

1. Mix together ingredients and chill.

Empanadas with Cajun Aioli SK

MAKES 24

- 1 sheet Puff Pastry
- 1/4 lb. Ground Breakfast Sausage
- 1/2 T Dried Minced Onions
- 1/4 t Garlic Powder

- 1/4 t Cumin
- 1/4 t Pumpkin Pie Spice
- 2 T Green/Calamata Olives, chopped
- 2 T Raisins, chopped

1. Preheat oven to 400°F. Thaw a sheet of Puff Pastry and roll out on a floured surface to approximately 11"x14".
2. With a pizza cutter cut sheet into 24 pieces (4 rows & 6 columns). Stretch pastry squares slightly and lay into cups of a mini muffin pan.
3. In a fry pan over medium heat, cook Sausage thoroughly and drain.
4. Add Minced Onions, Garlic Powder, Cumin, and Pumpkin Pie Spice to sausage.
5. Saute for 4 minutes. Remove from heat and add Olives and Raisins.
6. Fill each cup with 1 teaspoon of mixture and pinch corners of Pastry closed.
7. Bake for 12 - 15 minutes or until tops begin to brown. Serve with our Cajun Aioli (recipe below).

Cajun Aioli

- 1 C Mayonnaise
- 12 drops Tabasco Sauce
- 1/2 t Garlic Powder
- 1 T Chili Powder

- 1/2 T Dried Minced Onions
- 1/4 t Nutmeg
- 1/2 t Pepper

1. Mix ingredients together and chill.

Ham and Cheese Bites ⓈⓀ

MAKES 24

- 1 sheet Puff Pastry, thawed
- 1/4 C Ham, chopped into small cubes
- 1/4 C Cheddar Cheese, shredded

1. Preheat oven to 400°F. Thaw a sheet of Puff Pastry and roll out on a floured surface to approximately 11"x14".
2. With a pizza cutter cut sheet into 24 pieces (4 rows & 6 columns). Stretch pastry squares slightly and lay into cups of a mini muffin pan.
3. Fill each cup with 1 teaspoon Ham and top evenly with Cheese.
4. Bake for 12 - 15 minutes or until corners begin to brown.

Spinach and Feta Bites ⓈⓀ

MAKES 24

- 1 sheet Puff Pastry, thawed
- 1 T Olive Oil
- 1 T Dried Minced Onions
- 1/2 C Frozen Spinach, thawed and squeezed dry
- Salt (to taste)
- 1/8 t Pepper (or to taste)
- Feta Cheese

1. Preheat oven to 400°F. Thaw a sheet of Puff Pastry and roll out on a floured surface to approximately 11"x14".
2. With a pizza cutter cut sheet into 24 pieces (4 rows & 6 columns). Stretch pastry squares slightly and lay into cups of mini muffin pan.
3. Mix together Oil, Minced Onions, Spinach, Salt, and Pepper.
4. Fill each cup with 1 teaspoon of mixture and top evenly with Cheese.
5. Bake for 12 - 15 minutes or until corners begin to brown.

SALSAS

Delicious and healthy, these Salsas make a perfect starter with Tortilla Chips. Also, try them over grilled Chicken or Flank Steak as a fresh, tasty garnish.

Black Bean Mandarin Orange Salsa

SERVES 8

- 1 10 oz. can Mandarin Oranges, with juice
- 1/4 C Balsamic Vinegar
- 1/8 t Red Pepper Flakes (or to taste)
- 1/2 t Salt
- 1/4 t Pepper
- 1/4 C Olive Oil
- 1 15 oz. can Black Beans, drained and rinsed
- 1 Bell Pepper, chopped
- 1 Shallot or 1/4 medium Onion, diced
- 1/4 C Fresh Basil, chopped

1. Drain 1/3 C of juice from Mandarin Oranges and place juice in mixing bowl. Add Balsamic Vinegar, Red Pepper Flakes, Salt, and Pepper.
2. Whisk in Olive Oil until mixture is emulsified.
3. Drain and discard the rest of the juice from Mandarin Oranges. Chop up Mandarin Oranges and add to the bowl with remaining ingredients. Mix together well.
4. Chill for at least one hour. (It's even better if you chill overnight.) Serve with Tortilla Chips or over grilled meat.

46

Cucumber Thai Salsa

SERVES 8

- 1 t Salt
- 1 T Ginger
- 2 T White Wine Vinegar
- 2 T Honey
- 2 T Vegetable Oil

- 1 English Cucumber, chopped
- 1/4 C Bell Pepper, chopped
- 1/4 C Fresh Basil
- 3 T Peanuts, chopped

1. Mix ingredients in order, making sure to whisk in oil well to emulsify.
2. Chill for at least one hour. (It's even better if you chill overnight.) Serve with Tortilla Chips or over grilled meat.

MULTI-TASK YOUR RECIPES

A main objective of this system is to get the most out of the ingredients that you have in your home. The same philosophy applies to our recipes. We love using the same recipe in multiple ways and extending their benefits. These Salsas are a perfect example. They are delicious with tortilla chips or our Garlic Toast recipe, but also provide a fresh take on your grilled meats as a garnish. Take it a step further by marinating the meats and then topping with the salsa.

Try:
Asian Marinade with Cucumber Thai Salsa
Italian Marinade with Italian Salsa/Bruschetta
Honey Lime Marinade with Pineapple Tomato Salsa
Java Marinade with Black Bean Mandarin Orange Salsa

Italian Salsa / Bruschetta

SERVES 6

- 1 T Balsamic Vinegar
- 1/2 t Salt
- 1/4 t Pepper
- 2 cloves Garlic, minced

- 2 T Olive Oil
- 1 1/2 C Tomatoes, fresh, chopped or 1 15 oz. can Diced Tomatoes, drained
- 1/2 C Fresh Basil, chopped

1. Mix ingredients in order, making sure to whisk in oil well to emulsify.
2. Chill for at least one hour. (It's even better if you chill overnight.) Serve with our Garlic Toast (recipe below) or over grilled meat.

Garlic Toasts

SERVES 6

- 9 slices Bread, crusts removed
- 3 T Unsalted Butter, melted
- 1/2 t Garlic Powder

1. Preheat oven to 400°F.
2. Mix Butter and Garlic Powder and brush over slices. Cut slices into 4 triangles.
3. Bake at for 12 minutes.

48

Pineapple Tomato Salsa SK

SERVES 6

- 1 15 oz. can Pineapple, drain and reserve juice
- 2 T Lime Juice
- 1/4 t Salt
- 1/2 t Red Pepper Flakes (or to taste)
- 1 T Olive Oil
- 1 1/2 C Tomatoes, fresh, chopped or 1 15 oz. can Diced Tomatoes, drained
- 1/4 C Bell Pepper, chopped
- 2 T Shallot or 1/4 C Onion, finely diced
- 1/4 C Fresh Basil

1. Mix 1/3 C of reserved Pineapple juice, Lime Juice, Salt, Red Pepper Flakes together. Drizzle in Olive Oil while whisking to emulsify.
2. Chop Pineapple and add to Juice mixture along with remaining ingredients
3. Chill for at least one hour. (It's even better if you chill overnight.) Serve with Tortilla Chips or over grilled meat.

SAUSAGE MEATBALLS

These are wonderful, bite size starters for any occasion. Keep them warm at an event in a crock pot. We dedicate this section to Stacey's husband Craig, who not only loves these little balls of meat, but could eat the Ginger Sauce on a shoe!

Sausage Meatballs SK

MAKES 24

- 1 lb. Ground Breakfast Sausage
- 1/2 C Plain Bread Crumbs
- 2 T Dried Minced Onions
- 2 Eggs

1. Preheat oven to 375°F
2. Combine ingredients and form 1" meatballs. Place meatballs on a jelly roll pan lined with Aluminum Foil and topped with a nesting cooling rack.
3. Bake for 20 to 25 minutes. Meatballs can be made ahead and refrigerated or frozen to serve later.

Barbecue Sauce

- 1 1/2 C Barbecue Sauce
- 1/2 C Water

1. In saucepan over medium heat, mix ingredients together.
2. Add cooked meatballs and heat thoroughly.

Ginger Sauce

- 1 C Apricot Preserves
- 1/2 C Barbecue Sauce
- 1 T Ginger

1. In saucepan over medium heat, mix ingredients together.
2. Add cooked meatballs and heat thoroughly.

Raspberry Sauce

- 1 C Raspberry Jam
- 1/2 C Ketchup
- 1/4 C Brown Sugar

- 2 T White Wine Vinegar
- 1/2 t Pumpkin Pie Spice

1. In saucepan over medium heat, mix ingredients together.
2. Add cooked meatballs and heat thoroughly.

Teriyaki Sauce

- 1 15 oz. can Pineapple Chunks, drained
- 3 cloves Garlic, minced
- 1 T Ginger

- 1/3 C Soy Sauce
- 2 T White Wine Vinegar
- 1/4 t Red Pepper Flakes
- 3/4 C Brown Sugar

1. In saucepan over medium heat, mix ingredients together.
2. Add cooked meatballs and heat thoroughly.

SERVING MEATBALLS

Make sure to have appetizer plates and toothpicks available when serving these delicious, little balls of meat. They can get rather messy without them.

We always try to use real dishes instead of paper or plastic. They create a nicer presentation, stand up to heavier recipes, and cause much less waste.

TORTILLA ROLL-UPS

These are wonderful bite-size treats. Try the same technique as below with simple PB&J for a child friendly snack!

Greek Tortilla Roll-Ups

MAKES 48

- 1/2 C Green/Calamata Olives, finely chopped
- 1 T Lemon Juice
- 3/4 C English Cucumber, finely diced
- 1 C Sour Cream/Plain Yogurt
- 1 1/2 C Feta Cheese

- 1 8 oz. pkg. Cream Cheese
- 2 T Dried Minced Onions
- 1 t Dill Weed
- 1/2 t Garlic Powder
- 8 Flour Tortillas (8" or Fajita size)

1. Mix all ingredients, except Tortillas, in a mixing bowl.
2. Spread about 1/2 C of the mixture over one side of a Tortilla, close to edges. Roll Tortilla up tightly. Repeat with the remaining Tortillas and Cream Cheese mixture.
3. Wrap each tortilla individually in Plastic Wrap and refrigerate between 1 to 24 hours.
4. Cut each Tortilla into 1 inch slices.

Ham and Relish Tortilla Roll-Ups

MAKES 48

- 1/4 C Sour Cream/Plain Yogurt
- 1 8 oz. pkg. Cream Cheese, softened
- 1 C Ham, finely diced
- 1/2 C Sweet or Dill Relish
- 8 Flour Tortillas (8" or Fajita size)

1. Mix all ingredients, except Tortillas, in a mixing bowl.
2. Spread about 1/8 of the mixture over one side of a Tortilla, close to edges. Roll Tortilla up tightly. Repeat with the remaining Tortillas and Ham mixture.
3. Wrap each Tortilla individually in Plastic Wrap and refrigerate between 1 to 24 hours.
4. Cut each Tortilla into 1 inch slices.

54

Vegetable Tortilla Roll-Ups

MAKES 48

- 1/2 C Black Olives, finely chopped
- 3/4 C Bell Pepper, finely diced
- 1 C Sour Cream/Plain Yogurt
- 1 C Cheddar Cheese, shredded
- 1 8 oz. pkg. Cream Cheese
- 2 stalks Green Onions, finely sliced
- 8 Flour Tortillas (8" or Fajita size)

1. Mix all ingredients, except Tortillas, in a mixing bowl.
2. Spread about 1/2 C of the mixture over one side of a Tortilla, close to edges. Roll Tortilla up tightly. Repeat with the remaining Tortillas and Cream Cheese mixture.
3. Wrap each Tortilla individually in Plastic Wrap and refrigerate between 1 to 24 hours.
4. Cut each Tortilla into 1 inch slices.

Salads

tangy pear vinaigrette salad

parmesan crisps

chili lime coleslaw

carrot and raisin salad

mediterranean rice salad

apricot chicken salad

DRESSINGS AND PAIRINGS

One of the best parts of this system is the ability to make what you need when you need it. These salad dressings are a wonderful example of this. Eat what you want and only make what you need!

Balsamic Vinaigrette Salad

SERVES 4

DRESSING
- 1/4 C Balsamic Vinegar
- 1 T Shallot or Onion, diced (optional)
- 1 t Dijon Mustard
- 1/4 C Olive Oil

SALAD
- Lettuce/Mixed Greens
- Tomatoes
- Green Onions, thinly sliced
- Pine Nuts, toasted
- Parmesan Cheese

1. Whisk together Balsamic Vinegar, Shallot/Onion, and Dijon Mustard. Drizzle in Oil while whisking to emulsify.
2. On four plates layer SALAD ingredients. Drizzle with DRESSING. Try topped with grilled Chicken, grilled Flank Steak, or grilled or sauteed Shrimp.

TOASTING NUTS

Toasting nuts adds a tremendous amount of flavor to them because their natural oils are released. We like to toast nuts the following ways.
STOVE TOP: In a fry pan over medium heat, heat nuts in a dry pan until they are golden brown.
OVEN: Preheat oven to 350°F. On a Parchment Paper covered jelly roll pan, heat nuts for about 10 minutes or until golden brown.
The aroma of toasted nuts will let you know when they are done!

58

Basil Vinaigrette Salad

SERVES 4

DRESSING
- 1/4 C Lemon Juice
- 2 T Dijon Mustard
- 1/2 t Salt
- 1/4 t Pepper
- 1/3 C Olive Oil
- 1 1/2 C Fresh Basil, finely chopped

SALAD
- Lettuce/Mixed Greens
- Marinated Artichoke Hearts
- Green Onions, thinly sliced
- Green/Calamata Olives
- Hard Boiled Eggs
- Parmesan Cheese

1. Whisk together Lemon Juice, Dijon Mustard, Salt, and Pepper. Drizzle in Oil while whisking to emulsify. Stir in Basil.
2. On four plates layer SALAD ingredients. Drizzle with DRESSING. Try topped with grilled Chicken, grilled Flank Steak, or grilled or sauteed Shrimp.

BBQ Vinaigrette Salad

SERVES 4

DRESSING
- 1/4 C Red Wine Vinegar
- 1/4 C Barbecue Sauce
- 1/4 C Olive Oil

SALAD
- Lettuce/Mixed Greens
- Tomatoes
- Green Onions, thinly sliced
- Bleu/Gorgonzola Cheese
- Bell Pepper, diced

1. Whisk together Vinegar and Barbecue Sauce. Drizzle in Oil while whisking to emulsify.
2. On four plates layer SALAD ingredients. Drizzle with DRESSING.
3. Try topped with grilled Chicken, grilled Flank Steak, or grilled or sauteed Shrimp.

Caesar Salad

SERVES 4

DRESSING
- 1/2 C Mayonnaise
- 1/2 C Milk
- 1 T Lemon Juice
- 1 t Worcestershire
- 2 cloves Garlic, minced
- 1/4 t Salt
- 1/4 t Pepper
- 1/2 C Parmesan Cheese

SALAD
- Lettuce/Mixed Greens
- Tomatoes
- Croutons (see recipe below)

1. Whisk together all DRESSING ingredients. (If dressing is too thick, add Milk until it is the right consistency.)
2. On four plates layer SALAD ingredients. Drizzle with DRESSING.
3. Try topped with grilled Chicken, grilled Flank Steak, grilled or sauteed Shrimp, or diced Ham.

Croutons SK

- 2 slices Bread, cubed (extra bread from Frozen Bread Dough works great)
- 1 T Olive Oil
- 1/4 t Garlic Powder (optional)

1. Preheat oven to 400°F.
2. In a mixing bowl place cubed Bread, drizzle with Olive Oil, and sprinkle with Garlic Powder if desired. Toss together.
3. On a jelly roll pan, lay out cubed bread in a single layer and bake for 10 minutes or until crisp on outside.

60

Catalina Salad

SERVES 4

DRESSING
- 1/2 C Ketchup
- 2 T Sugar
- 2 T White Wine Vinegar
- 1/2 t Salt
- 2 T Dried Minced Onions
- 1/3 C Vegetable Oil

SALAD
- Lettuce/Mixed Greens
- Green Onions, thinly sliced
- Celery, diced
- Carrots, diced
- Frozen Peas, thawed
- Corn

1. Whisk together Ketchup, Sugar, Vinegar, Salt, and Dried Minced Onions. Drizzle in Oil while whisking to emulsify.
2. On four plates layer SALAD ingredients. Drizzle with DRESSING.
3. To make this a meal, serve this salad topped with grilled Chicken, grilled Flank Steak, grilled or sauteed Shrimp, diced Ham, or Crab Meat.

Creamy Cucumber Salad

SERVES 4

DRESSING
- 1/4 C Sour Cream/Plain Yogurt
- 1/4 C Milk
- 1/3 C English Cucumber, finely chopped
- 2 T Mayonnaise
- 2 T Green Onions, thinly sliced
- 2 T Lemon Juice
- 1/4 t Salt
- 1/4 t Dill Weed
- 1/8 t Pepper

SALAD
- Lettuce/Mixed Greens
- Bacon, cooked and crumbled
- Cheddar Cheese
- Frozen Peas, thawed
- Tomatoes, diced

1. Whisk together all DRESSING ingredients.
2. On four plates layer SALAD ingredients. Drizzle with DRESSING.
3. Try topped with grilled Chicken, grilled Flank Steak, grilled or sauteed Shrimp, or diced Ham.

62

Ginger Salad SK

SERVES 4

DRESSING
- 1 T Ginger
- 1 t Dried Minced Onions
- 2 T White Wine Vinegar
- 2 T Mayonnaise
- 1 T Soy Sauce
- 1/4 C Vegetable Oil

SALAD
- Lettuce/Mixed Greens
- Green Onions, thinly sliced
- Mandarin Oranges
- Almonds, toasted
- Cabbage and Carrot Mix

1. Whisk together Ginger, Dried Minced Onions, Vinegar, Mayonnaise, and Soy Sauce. Drizzle in Oil while whisking to emulsify.
2. On four plates layer SALAD ingredients. Drizzle with DRESSING. Try topped with grilled Chicken, grilled Flank Steak, or grilled or sauteed Shrimp.

Greek Salad SK

SERVES 4

DRESSING
- 1/4 C Lemon Juice
- 1 T Italian Seasoning
- 1 clove Garlic, minced
- 1/2 t Salt
- Pepper (to taste)
- 1/3 C Olive Oil

SALAD
- Lettuce/Mixed Greens
- English Cucumber, chopped
- Black Olives
- Artichoke Hearts, drained
- Roasted Red Peppers
- Feta Cheese

1. Whisk together Lemon Juice, Italian Seasoning, Garlic, Salt, and Pepper. Drizzle in Oil while whisking to emulsify.
2. On four plates layer SALAD ingredients. Drizzle with DRESSING. Try topped with grilled Chicken, grilled Flank Steak, or grilled or sauteed Shrimp.

Honey Apricot Salad

SERVES 4

DRESSING
- 1/4 C Apricot Preserves
- 1 C Sour Cream/Plain Yogurt
- 1/4 C Honey
- 1 T Lemon Juice
- 1/4 t Cinnamon

SALAD
- Lettuce/Mixed Greens
- Frozen Peas, thawed
- Mandarin Oranges
- Bleu/Gorgonzola Cheese
- Sugared Nuts (see recipe below)

1. Whisk together all DRESSING ingredients.
2. On four plates layer SALAD ingredients. Drizzle with DRESSING.
3. Try topped with grilled Chicken, grilled Flank Steak, grilled or sauteed Shrimp, or diced Ham.

Sugared Nuts SK

- 1/4 C Sugar
- 1/2 C Almonds, Pecans, or Peanuts

1. Over medium heat in fry pan, stir Sugar and Nuts until Sugar is melted and Nuts are coated.
2. Toss hot Nuts onto a sheet of Parchment Paper and allow to cool.
3. Once cool, break apart Nuts to separate.

64

Honey Mustard Salad

SERVES 4

DRESSING
- 1/2 C Mayonnaise
- 1/4 C Milk
- 2 T Yellow Mustard
- 2 T Honey
- 1 t Lemon Juice

SALAD
- Lettuce/Mixed Greens
- Frozen Peas, thawed
- Hard Boiled Eggs, chopped
- Tomatoes, diced
- Cheddar Cheese, shredded
- Bacon, cooked and chopped

1. Whisk together all DRESSING ingredients.
2. On four plates layer SALAD ingredients. Drizzle with DRESSING.
3. Try topped with grilled Chicken, grilled Flank Steak, or diced Ham.

THAT'S A WRAP!
Many of these Salads can also make great wraps, particularly this Honey Mustard Salad. Place Salad ingredients in a Flour Tortilla (or Pita), top with some grilled Chicken, and drizzle with Honey Mustard dressing. Wrap like a burrito and enjoy a delicious snack or lunch!

Italian Vinaigrette Salad

SERVES 4

DRESSING
- 1/4 C Red Wine Vinegar
- 1 T Water
- 2 t Sugar
- 1 t Lemon Juice
- 1/2 t Garlic Powder
- 1/2 t Salt
- 1 t Minced Onions
- 1/4 t Pepper
- 1 T Italian Seasoning
- 1/4 C Olive Oil

SALAD
- Lettuce/Mixed Greens
- Tomatoes, diced
- Bell Pepper, diced
- Black Olives
- Green Onions, thinly sliced
- Parmesan Crisp Recipe

1. Whisk together all Vinegar, Water, Sugar, Lemon Juice, Garlic Powder, Salt, Minced Onions, Pepper, and Italian Seasoning. Drizzle in Oil while whisking to emulsify.
2. On four plates layer SALAD ingredients. Drizzle with DRESSING.
3. To make this a meal, serve this salad topped with grilled Chicken, grilled Flank Steak, or grilled or sauteed Shrimp.

Parmesan Crisps SK

- 2 C Parmesan Cheese
- 2 t Herbes de Provence

- 1/4 t Black Pepper

1. Preheat oven to 350°F.
2. In a mixing bowl, mix together Cheese, Herbes de Provence, and Pepper. On a jelly roll pan covered with Parchment Paper, spoon a tablespoon of mixture. Press mound down flat. Keep approximately 4 inches between crisps.
3. Bake for 4 – 5 minutes until just golden brown. Cool completely and serve.

66

Raspberry Vinaigrette Salad SK

SERVES 4

DRESSING
- 3 T Raspberry Jam/Jelly
- 3 T Balsamic Vinegar
- 1 t Dijon Mustard
- 3 T Olive Oil

SALAD
- Lettuce/Mixed Greens
- Green Onions, thinly sliced
- Bleu/Gorgonzola Cheese
- Pears or Apples, chopped
- Dried Cranberries
- Sugared Nuts

1. Whisk together all Raspberry Jam/Jelly, Balsamic Vinegar, and Dijon Mustard. Drizzle in Oil while whisking to emulsify.
2. On four plates layer SALAD ingredients. Drizzle with DRESSING.
3. To make this a meal, serve this salad topped with grilled Chicken, grilled Flank Steak, grilled or sauteed Shrimp, or Ham.

Sugared Nuts SK

- 1/4 C Sugar
- 1/2 C Almonds, Pecans, or Peanuts

1. Over medium heat in fry pan, stir Sugar and Nuts until Sugar is melted and Nuts are coated.
2. Toss hot Nuts onto a sheet of Parchment Paper and allow to cool.
3. Once cool, break apart Nuts to separate.

Salsa Ranch Salad

SERVES 4

DRESSING
- 1/2 C Ranch Dressing
- 1/4 C Salsa

SALAD
- Lettuce/Mixed Greens
- Tomatoes, chopped
- Kidney Beans, drained and rinsed
- Corn, drained
- Green Onions, thinly sliced
- Cheddar Cheese, shredded
- Tortilla Chips

1. Whisk together all DRESSING ingredients.
2. On four plates layer SALAD ingredients. Drizzle with DRESSING. Try topped with grilled Chicken, grilled Flank Steak, or our Taco Meat recipe.

Simple Bleu Cheese Salad

SERVES 4

DRESSING
- 1/2 C Ranch Dressing
- 1/4 C Bleu/Gorgonzola Cheese

SALAD
- Lettuce/Mixed Greens
- Tomatoes, chopped
- Bell Peppers, diced
- Carrots, chopped
- Green Onions, thinly sliced

1. Whisk together all DRESSING ingredients.
2. On four plates layer SALAD ingredients. Drizzle with DRESSING. Try topped with grilled Chicken, grilled Flank Steak, or Ham.

68

Tangy Pear Vinaigrette Salad

SERVES 4

DRESSING
- 1/2 15 oz. can Pears, drained
- 1/2 C White Wine Vinegar
- 1 T Shallot, minced or 1 T Dried Minced Onions
- 1/4 t Garlic Powder
- 3 T Honey
- 1/4 t Salt
- 1/8 t Pepper
- 1/2 C Vegetable Oil
- 1 t Dijon Mustard

SALAD
- Lettuce/Mixed Greens
- Apples, chopped
- Dried Cranberries
- Pine Nuts
- Bacon, cooked and chopped

1. Blend together all DRESSING ingredients in a blender until smooth.
2. On four plates layer SALAD ingredients. Drizzle with DRESSING.
3. To make this a meal, serve this salad topped with grilled Chicken, grilled Flank Steak, or grilled or sauteed Shrimp.

COLESLAWS

These coleslaws are not only delicious, quick, and easy side dishes, they are a wonderful way to use up Cabbage and Carrot Mix!

Asian Vinaigrette Coleslaw

SERVES 6

- 1/4 C Sugar
- 2 T Soy Sauce
- 1/2 C Red Wine Vinegar
- 1/2 C Vegetable Oil
- 4 C Cabbage and Carrot Mix

1. Whisk together all ingredients, besides the Cabbage and Carrot Mix, in mixing bowl until well combined.
2. Add Cabbage and Carrot Mix and toss to coat. Cover and refrigerate for at least an hour before serving.

Chili Lime Coleslaw SK

SERVES 6

- 3/4 C Mayonnaise
- 1/4 C Sour Cream/Plain Yogurt
- 1/4 C Milk
- 1/4 C Lime Juice
- 2 t Chili Powder
- 1 t Cumin
- 1 T Sugar
- 4 C Cabbage and Carrot Mix

1. Whisk together all ingredients, besides the Cabbage and Carrot Mix, in mixing bowl until well combined.
2. Add Cabbage and Carrot Mix and toss to coat. Cover and refrigerate for at least an hour before serving.

Traditional/Dill Coleslaw

SERVES 6

- 3/4 C Mayonnaise
- 3/4 C Milk
- 3 T White Wine Vinegar
- 3 T Sugar
- 1 T Dijon Mustard
- 1 t Dill Weed (optional)
- 4 C Cabbage and Carrot Mix

1. Whisk together all ingredients, besides the Cabbage and Carrot Mix, in mixing bowl until well combined.
2. Add Cabbage and Carrot Mix and toss to coat. Cover and refrigerate for at least an hour before serving.

PICNIC SALADS

As this title implies, these salads are perfect for warm summer BBQs. What it doesn't imply are the little twists that make these recipes special, delicious, and perfect for any occasion.

Carrot and Raisin Salad

SERVES 4 - 6

- 1 15 oz. can Pineapple Chunks, with juice
- 1 T Cinnamon
- 2 T Lime Juice
- 1/2 C Sour Cream/Plain Yogurt
- 4 C Carrots, peeled and shredded
- 1 C Raisins

1. Drain 1/4 C Pineapple Juice into a mixing bowl. Whisk together Pineapple Juice with Cinnamon, Lime Juice, and Sour Cream/Plain Yogurt.
2. Drain remaining juice from Pineapple. Toss Sour Cream mixture with Carrots, Raisins, and remaining Pineapple.
3. Chill for at least 1 hour before serving.

72

Crab Macaroni Salad

SERVES 4 - 6

- 6 oz. - 1/2 lb. Penne Pasta, cooked and cooled
- 1/3 C Mayonnaise
- 1/3 C Sour Cream/Plain Yogurt
- 2 T Milk
- 2 T Sugar
- 1/4 t Nutmeg
- 1/2 t Salt
- 1/8 t Pepper
- 1/2 C Peas, Thawed
- 4 Eggs, Hardboiled (optional)
- 1/4 C Green Onions, finely sliced
- 1/2 C Carrot, shredded
- 1 6 oz. pkg. Crab Meat, imitation (chopped) or canned lump (drained)

1. Whisk together Mayonnaise, Sour Cream/Plain Yogurt, Milk, Sugar, Nutmeg, Salt, and Pepper.
2. Toss remaining ingredients with dressing. Chill for at least one hour before serving.

Ginger Pasta Salad

SERVES 4

- 1 T Ginger
- 1 t Dried Minced Onions
- 2 T White Wine Vinegar
- 2 T Mayonnaise
- 1 T Soy Sauce
- 1/4 C Vegetable Oil
- 1/2 lb. Thin Pasta, cooked, drained, and cooled
- 3 Green Onions, thinly sliced
- 1 10 oz. can Mandarin Oranges, drained
- 1/2 C Almonds, toasted
- 1 C Cabbage and Carrot Mix

1. Whisk together Ginger, Dried Minced Onions, Vinegar, Mayonnaise, and Soy Sauce. Drizzle in Oil while whisking to emulsify.
2. Toss remaining ingredients into dressing. Chill at least one hour before serving.

Greek Pasta Salad SK

SERVES 4

- 1/4 C Lemon Juice
- 1 T Italian Seasoning
- 1 clove Garlic, minced
- 1/2 t Salt
- Pepper (to taste)
- 1/3 C Olive Oil
- 6 oz. - 1/2 lb. Penne Pasta, cooked, drained, and cooled
- 1 C English Cucumber, chopped
- 1/2 C Black Olives, sliced or chopped
- 1 C Artichoke Hearts, drained
- 2 Roasted Red Peppers
- 3/4 C Feta Cheese

1. Whisk together Lemon Juice, Italian Seasoning, Garlic, Salt, and Pepper. Drizzle in Oil while whisking to emulsify.
2. Toss remaining ingredients into dressing. Chill at least one hour before serving.

74

Italian Pasta Salad

SERVES 4

- 1/4 C Red Wine Vinegar
- 1 T Water
- 2 t Sugar
- 1 t Lemon Juice
- 1/2 t Garlic Powder
- 1/2 t Salt
- 1 t Minced Onions
- 1/4 t Pepper
- 1 T Italian Seasoning
- 1/4 C Olive Oil
- 6 oz. - 1/2 lb. Penne Pasta, cooked, drained, and cooled
- 1/2 Bell Pepper, diced
- 1 Tomatoes, diced
- 2 Carrots, chopped
- 2 stalks Celery, chopped
- 1 C English Cucumber, diced
- 3 Green Onions, thinly sliced

1. Whisk together all Vinegar, Water, Sugar, Lemon Juice, Garlic Powder, Salt, Minced Onions, Pepper, and Italian Seasoning. Drizzle in Oil while whisking to emulsify.
2. Toss remaining ingredients into dressing. Chill at least one hour before serving.

Mediterranean Rice Salad SK

SERVES 4 - 6

- 1 C Rice
- 1 15 oz. can or 2 C Chicken Broth
- 1/4 C Lemon Juice
- 2 cloves Garlic, minced
- 1 t Salt
- 1/4 C Olive Oil
- 1 15-oz. can Northern/Cannelini Beans, rinsed well and drained
- 3/4 C Feta Cheese
- 1 Roasted Red Pepper, diced
- 1/2 C Fresh Basil
- 1 t Dill Weed
- 3 Green Onions, very thinly sliced

1. In a saucepan bring Rice and Broth to a boil, reduce heat, cover and simmer for approximately 30 minutes or until liquid is absorbed. Remove from heat and cool.
2. While the Rice is cooling whisk together Lemon Juice, Garlic, and Salt. Gradually drizzle in Oil while whisking to emulsify.
3. Toss with remaining ingredients and chill for at least 1 hour before serving.

76

Salsa Ranch Pasta Salad

SERVES 4

- 1/2 C Ranch Dressing
- 1/4 C Salsa
- 6 oz. - 1/2 lb. Penne Pasta, cooked, drained, and cooled
- Tomatoes, chopped
- 1 15 oz. can Kidney Beans, drained and rinsed
- 1 15 oz. can Corn, drained
- 3 Green Onions, thinly sliced
- 1 C Cheddar Cheese, shredded
- Tortilla Chips, crushed

1. Whisk together Ranch Dressing and Salsa.
2. Toss remaining Pasta, Beans, Corn, Green Onions, and Cheddar Cheese into dressing. Chill at least one hour.
3. Sprinkle with crushed Tortilla Chips and serve.

Tangy Potato Salad

SERVES 4 - 6

- 5 lbs. of Potatoes, peeled
- 4-6 Eggs
- 1 Shallot or 1/4 Onion, finely diced
- 1 T Sweet or Dill Relish
- 1 C Mayonnaise
- 2 T White Wine Vinegar
- 2 T Sugar
- 1/4 C Ketchup
- 2 T Olive Oil
- 1/2 t Garlic Powder
- 1 t Worcestershire Sauce
- 1 t Salt
- 1/2 t Pepper

1. In one stock pot combine Potatoes (unpeeled) and Eggs. Cover with water and bring to a boil over medium high heat. Reduce heat and simmer.
2. Remove Eggs after 15 minutes and place in ice bath to cool. Remove Potatoes after they are fork tender. Let Potatoes and Eggs cool. Peel and dice all Potatoes and Eggs.
3. Whisk together all other ingredients. Toss gently with Potatoes and Eggs. Chill for at least 3 hours before serving. (Can make a day ahead.)

SANDWICH SALADS

Any of these delicious salads can be served on a bed of Mixed Greens, in Pita Bread, on Bread, or as a wrap in a Tortilla.

Apricot Chicken Salad SK

SERVES 4

- 1/2 lb. Boneless, Skinless Chicken, cooked and cubed
- 2 T Almonds, slivered or chopped
- 2 T Celery Stalk, chopped
- 2 T Mayonnaise
- 2 T Apricot Preserves
- 1/2 t Herbes De Provence
- 1/2 T Dijon Mustard
- 1/4 t Salt
- 1/8 t Pepper

1. Mix all ingredients well. Chill and serve.

THE ROTISSERIE CHICKEN

Although a Rotisserie Chicken is not on our list, we like to pick one up on the day that we shop and use it for recipes that require cooked and chopped or shredded Chicken. It is a great way to cut out one step.

Egg Salad

SERVES 4

- 6 Eggs, hardboiled, chopped
- 2 T Celery, finely minced
- 1 1/2 T Sweet or Dill Relish
- 1/4 C Mayonnaise
- 1 t Dried Minced Onions
- 1 t Yellow Mustard
- 1/2 t Salt
- 1/4 t Pepper

1. Mix together ingredients. Chill and serve.

Ham Salad

SERVES 4

- 2 C Ham
- 3 T Mayonnaise
- 1 t Yellow Mustard
- 1/2 t Honey
- 1 T Sweet or Dill Relish
- 1/8 t Pepper

1. In a food processor grind Ham and blend with remaining ingredients. If a food processor is not available, finely dice Ham and mix with remaining ingredients.
2. Chill and serve.

HAM IT UP!
Ham Salad might, at first, sound a bit old fashioned. We think this recipe is just the opposite. Not only is it a quick and easy lunch, it makes a wonderful dip with crackers. Try serving it in a bowl topped with chopped Green or Black Olives.

80

Seafood Salad

SERVES 4

- 1 C Shrimp, peeled, de-veined, de-tailed, cooked, and chopped
- 1 6 oz. pkg. Crab Meat, imitation (chopped) or canned lump (drained)
- 1/4 C Mayonnaise

- 1/4 C Ranch Dressing
- 2 T Lemon Juice
- 1/2 t Dill Weed
- 1/4 C Green Onion, thinly sliced
- 1/2 C Bell Pepper, diced

1. Mix together ingredients. Chill and serve.

Traditional Chicken Salad

SERVES 4

- 1/2 lb. Boneless Skinless Chicken, cooked and cubed
- 2/3 C Mayonnaise
- 1 t Sugar

- 1/2 t Salt
- 1/4 t Pepper
- 1/2 T Dried Minced Onions
- 1 T Sweet or Dill Relish (optional)

1. Mix all ingredients well. Chill and serve.

CHICKEN SALAD OPTION

We like to enhance the flavor in our Traditional Chicken Salad by mixing in the following:
- 1/4 C Nuts
- 1/4 C Raisins or Dried Cranberries
- 1/2 C Apples, cored, peeled, and diced

Soups and Breads

SOUPS, STEWS, AND CHILIS

BREADS

carrot and bleu cheese soup

vichyssoise

gaspacho

italian stew

ham, corn, and potato chowder

cheesy chicken chili

SOUPS, STEWS, AND CHILIS

Nothing is more comforting on a cold winter's day than a great tasting soup.
We love this section, also, for the cold soups that are great warm weather
options. Most of these soups freeze wonderfully!

Asian Black Bean Chili

SERVES 6

- 2 T Olive Oil
- 1 C Shallot or 2 C Onion, chopped
- 2 cloves Garlic
- 2 T Chili Powder
- 1 t Cumin
- 1/2 t Cinnamon
- 3 15 oz. cans Black Beans, drained
- 2 15 oz. cans Diced Tomatoes, undrained
- 1 C Mandarin Oranges, drained and chopped
- 2 t Salt
- 2 T Honey

1. Heat Olive Oil in stock pot over medium heat.
2. Add Shallots/Onions and Garlic. Cook until vegetables are softened.
3. Stir in Chili Powder, Cumin, and Cinnamon.
4. Stir in Black Beans, Diced Tomatoes, Mandarin Oranges, and Salt and bring to a
   boil. Reduce heat and add Honey. Simmer covered for 30 minutes, stirring often.

84

Carrot and Bleu Cheese Soup (Cold)

SERVES 6

- 1 T Olive Oil
- 3 C Carrots, chopped
- 1/2 C Shallot or 1 C Onion, diced
- 2 cloves, Garlic
- 1 t Herbes De Provence
- 1 15 oz. can or 2 C Chicken Broth
- 1 1/2 t Salt
- 1/4 C Sour Cream/Plain Yogurt
- 1/2 C Bleu/Gorgonzola Cheese (or to taste)

1. In a stock pot heat Oil over medium heat. Add Carrots, Shallots/Onions, and Garlic and cook until vegetables are very soft. Add Herbes de Provence, Broth, and Salt and bring to a boil. Reduce heat and simmer for about 15 minutes.
2. Remove from heat and let cool. Puree mixture in blender or food processor (in batches if necessary) until mixture is smooth. Chill for several hours.
3. Before serving, swirl in a tablespoon of Sour Cream/Yogurt and top with Bleu Cheese.

Cheese Soup SK

SERVES 6

- 1 15 oz. can or 2 C Chicken Broth
- 1/2 C Carrot, shredded
- 1/4 C Celery, shredded
- 1/4 C Onion, shredded (or 1 T Dried Minced Onions)
- 1 3/4 C Milk
- 1/3 C Flour
- Dash Pepper
- 1 1/2 C Cheddar Cheese

1. In a medium saucepan combine Chicken Broth, Carrot, Celery, and Onion.
2. Bring to a boil, reduce heat, and simmer for 8 minutes or until vegetables are tender. In a separate bowl, whisk together Milk, Flour, and Pepper.
3. Stir the milk mixture into the Chicken Broth and cook and stir until thick and bubbly.
4. Add in Cheddar Cheese and stir until melted.

86

Cheesy Chicken Chili

SERVES 6

- 1.5 lb. Boneless Skinless Chicken
- 2 T Olive Oil
- 4 15 oz. cans Beans, White or Cannellini
- 1 15 oz. can or 2 C Chicken Broth
- 2 C Salsa
- 1 t Cumin
- 2 C Cheddar Cheese

1. Cut Chicken Breasts into 1" cubes. In stock pot over medium heat, cook Chicken in Olive Oil until no longer pink inside.
2. Stir in Beans, Chicken Broth, Salsa, and Cumin.
3. Bring to a boil and then reduce heat to a simmer for 30 minutes, stirring occasionally.
4. Add Cheddar Cheese and stir until cheese is completely melted.
5. If desired, top with Cheddar Cheese and Sour Cream, and serve with Tortilla Chips.

Chicken Noodle Soup

SERVES 6

- 1 lb. Boneless Skinless Chicken
- 1 T Olive Oil
- 1/2 C Onion, chopped (or 2 T Dried Minced Onions)
- 1/2 C Celery, chopped
- 1/2 C Carrots, chopped
- 2 15 oz. cans or 4 C Chicken Broth
- 4 C Hot Water
- 1/4 t Pepper
- 1/2 t Salt
- 1 C Egg Noodles
- 1/2 C Frozen Peas

1. Cut Chicken into 1 inch pieces and set aside. In stock pot, heat Oil over medium heat, add Onion, and cook for 5 minutes.
2. Add Celery, Carrots, Chicken Broth, Hot Water, Salt, and Pepper. Cover and heat to boiling over high heat.
3. Add Egg Noodles. Cover and cook for an additional 3 minutes.
4. Stir in uncooked Chicken pieces and Peas. Cover and heat to boiling again. Simmer for 10 minutes.

88

Creamy Broccoli Soup

SERVES 6

- 3 T Olive Oil
- 1 C Carrots, chopped
- 1 C Celery, chopped
- 3/4 C Onions, chopped (or 2 T Dried Minced Onions)
- 2 15 oz. cans or 4 C Chicken Broth
- 1/2 t Pepper
- 4 1/2 C Broccoli, chopped
- 1/2 C Rice
- 2 C Milk
- 1/4 C Parmesan Cheese

1. Heat Olive Oil in a large saucepan. Add Carrots, Celery, and Onions and cook for 5 minutes. Add Chicken Broth and Pepper. Stir and bring to a boil.
2. Stir in Broccoli and Rice. Reduce heat and simmer for 30 minutes.
3. In 1 cup increments, add soup to blender or food processor and blend until pureed.
4. Return to saucepan and add Milk and Cheese. Cook until heated through.

Gaspacho (Cold)

SERVES 6

- 3 Tomatoes, diced or 1 15 oz. can Diced Tomatoes
- 1 15 oz. can Tomato Sauce
- 2 T Shallots or 1/4 C Onion, diced
- 1/2 English Cucumber, diced
- 1/2 Bell Pepper, seeded and diced
- 2 stalks Celery, chopped
- 2 T Fresh Basil, chopped
- 1 cloves Garlic, minced
- 1 T Balsamic Vinegar
- 1 t Worcestershire Sauce
- 2 T Olive Oil
- 1 t Salt
- 1/4 t Pepper

1. Add all ingredients to blender and pulse until it has a blended consistency.
2. Chill 1 to 24 hours and serve cold.

WHAT IS GASPACHO?
Gaspacho is a cold Spanish soup made from tomatoes and other raw vegetables. It is delicious, easy, and completely satisfying on a hot summer's day! Try topped with sour cream and served with our Garlic Toast recipe.

90

Ham, Potato, and Corn Chowder SK

SERVES 6

- 3 lbs. Potatoes, pealed and cubed
- 3 15 oz. cans Corn
- 2 T Unsalted Butter
- 1/2 C Shallot or 1 C Onion, diced
- 3 stalks Celery, diced
- 2 T Flour
- 3 C Milk
- 1 15 oz. can or 2 C Chicken Broth
- 1 t Herbs de Provence
- 12 dashes Tabasco/Hot Sauce
- 1 T Salt
- 2 C Ham, diced
- 1 C Sour Cream/Plain Yogurt

1. Peel and cube Potatoes and set aside. Blend 2 cans of Corn until smooth.
2. In a stock pot melt Butter over medium heat. Add Shallot or Onion and Celery and cook until vegetables are tender. Sprinkle with Flour and stir until blended.
3. Gradually add Milk and then Broth while stirring. Bring to a boil and cook for about 3 minutes.
4. Add reserve Potatoes and blended Corn. Bring back up to a boil and cook for 10 minutes.
5. Drain last can of Corn and add along with remaining ingredients. Simmer for 20 minutes. Serve with Sour Cream.

Italian Stew SK

SERVES 6

- 1 lb. Ground Beef or Ground Breakfast Sausage
- 1/2 C Shallots or 1 C Onion, diced
- 1 C Celery, chopped
- 1 C Carrots, chopped
- 2 cloves Garlic, minced
- 1 15 oz. can Diced Tomatoes
- 1 15 oz. can Tomato Sauce
- 1 15 oz. can Kidney Beans, undrained

- 1 15 oz. can or 2 C Beef Broth
- 1 T Italian Seasonings
- 2 T Fresh Basil, chopped
- 1 t Salt
- 1/4 t Pepper
- 2 C Cabbage and Carrot Mix
- 1 C Frozen Green Beans
- 1 C Penne Pasta or Egg Noodles

1. In a stock pot over medium heat, cook Ground Beef or Sausage thoroughly. Drain meat and return pot to stove top.
2. Add Shallots or Onion, Celery, Carrots, and Garlic. Cook over medium heat until vegetables soften.
3. Add to pot Diced Tomatoes, Tomato Sauce, Kidney Beans, Beef Broth, Italian Seasonings, Basil, Salt, and Pepper. Bring to a boil, cover, and reduce heat to a simmer for 30 minutes.
4. Add Cabbage and Carrot Mix, Green Beans, and Noodles. Bring back to a boil and cook for 10 minutes. Serve topped with Parmesan Cheese.

A HEARTY, HEALTHY MEAL

This stew is a wonderful make-ahead meal, and we use it as a way to sneak a lot of vegetables into our children! (Just sprinkle with parmesan cheese!)

This stew is also a great meal for guests. Serve with our Garlic Parmesan Roll-Up Bread recipe (at the end of this section) for a simple and more than satisfying meal!

92

Mom's Basic Chili

SERVES 6

- 1 lb. Ground Beef
- 2 Shallots or 1/2 large Onion, diced
- 1 Bell Pepper, diced
- 2 15 oz. Kidney Beans
- 1 15 oz. Tomato Sauce
- 2 15 oz. cans Diced Tomatoes
- 2 15 oz. cans or 4 C Beef Broth
- 2 T Chili Powder
- 1 T Cumin
- 1/2 t Tabasco/Hot Sauce (or to taste)
- 1 t Garlic Powder
- 1/2 t Salt
- 1/2 t Pepper

1. In a stock pot, brown Ground Beef. Drain and return over medium heat. Add Shallots or Onions and Bell Pepper. Cook until vegetables are softened.
2. Add Kidney Beans (with liquid), Tomato Sauce, Diced Tomatoes, and Beef Broth. Stir in Chili Powder, Cumin, Tabasco, Garlic Powder, Salt, and Pepper. Bring to a boil.
3. Reduce heat and simmer for at least 30 minutes. Simmering longer will enhance the flavors.
4. Try serving with Sour Cream and Cheddar Cheese.

Roasted Red Pepper Bisque

SERVES 6

- 1 T Olive Oil
- 2 Shallots (or 1/2 Cup Onion chopped)
- 2 15 oz. cans Diced Tomatoes (or 4 C Tomatoes, diced)
- 3 large Roasted Red Peppers, chopped
- 2 cloves Garlic, minced
- 1 t Italian Seasoning
- 1 t Salt
- 1/2 t Pepper
- 1 15 oz. can or 2 C Chicken Broth
- 1 T Sugar
- 1 T Fresh Basil, chopped
- 1/4 C Sour Cream/Plain Yogurt

1. In a stock pot, heat Oil over medium heat and saute Shallots or Onions until translucent.
2. Add Diced Tomatoes, Roasted Red Peppers, Garlic, Italian Seasonings, Salt, Pepper, and Chicken Broth.
3. Bring to a boil and simmer for 10 minutes. Add Sugar and Basil.
4. Transfer soup to a blender and puree.
5. Place back into stock pot. Cook 5 minutes more.
6. Remove from heat and whisk in Sour Cream.

MAKE THESE SOUPS VEGETARIAN
Many of these soups are veggie based. Don't forget, however, that to make them truly vegetarian, you need to substitute chicken or beef broth for vegetable broth. Although vegetable broth isn't on the list, it is readily available and can be substituted any time for chicken or beef broth.

94

Shrimp Bisque

SERVES 6

- 2 15 oz. cans or 4 C Chicken Broth
- 1 T Unsalted Butter
- 1/4 C Onion, chopped (or 1 shallot)
- 1/4 C Celery, chopped
- 1/4 C Carrots, chopped
- 1 15 oz. can Diced Tomatoes (or 1 1/2 C fresh Tomatoes diced)
- 4 T Rice, uncooked
- 1 T Olive Oil
- 12 oz. - 1 lb. Shrimp, raw, peeled, de-veined, and de-tailed
- 2 T Unsalted Butter, softened
- 1 C Heavy/Whipping Cream
- 1/4 t Salt
- 1/4 t Pepper

1. Over medium heat, heat Chicken Broth in a stock pot.
2. While Broth is heating, in a skillet, sauté Onion, Celery, and Carrots in 1 tablespoon of Unsalted Butter for 5 minutes.
3. Add Diced Tomatoes to the skillet and sauté for another 5 minutes.
4. Add mixture to the heated Chicken Broth. Stir in the Rice and return to a boil. Simmer partially covered for 20 minutes.
5. In the skillet used for the vegetables, heat the Olive Oil. Add Shrimp and cook until pink. Remove from skillet and set aside.
6. When soup is finished cooking, puree 1/2 of the cooked Shrimp and all of the soup in a blender and then return it to the saucepan.
7. Whisk into the soup the softened Unsalted Butter, Cream, Salt, and Pepper.
8. Let stand 5-10 minutes until ready to serve.
9. Ladle the soup into bowls and top with remaining Shrimp.

Shrimp Chili

SERVES 6

- 2 T Unsalted Butter
- 1 C Shallot or 2 C Onion, chopped
- 1 C Carrots, chopped
- 1 C Celery, chopped
- 3 cloves Garlic, minced
- 1/2 C Roasted Red pepper, diced
- 1 T Italian Seasonings
- 1 T Chili Powder
- 1 t Cumin
- 2 15 oz. cans Diced Tomatoes, undrained
- 2 15 oz. cans Kidney Beans, undrained
- 1 15 oz. can or 2 C Chicken Broth
- 2 t Salt
- 1 T Worcestershire Sauce
- Tabasco/Hot Sauce (to taste)
- 12 oz. - 1 lb. Shrimp, raw, peeled, de-veined, and de-tailed

1. Heat Unsalted Butter in stock pot over medium heat.
2. Add Shallots or Onions, Carrots, Celery, and Garlic and cook until vegetables are softened.
3. Stir in remaining ingredients, except for Shrimp and bring to a boil.
4. Reduce heat and simmer, uncovered, for 20 minutes, stirring occasionally.
5. Cut Shrimp in half and add to pot, cover, and cook for 10 minutes more.

96

Steak, Potato, and Corn Chili

SERVES 6

- 1 T Vegetable Oil
- 1 lb. Flank Steak, pound to tenderize and cut into 1/2" cubes
- 1 T Flour
- 1/2 C Shallot or 1 C Onion, diced
- 1 Bell Pepper, diced
- 1 clove Garlic, minced
- 3 T Chili Powder
- 1 t Cumin
- 2 15 oz. cans Diced Tomatoes, with juice
- 1 15 oz. can or 2 C Beef Broth
- 5 medium Potatoes (or 1.5 lbs.), peeled and cut in 1/2" cubes
- 1 15 oz. can Corn, drained
- 2 t Salt

1. Heat Vegetable Oil in stock pot over medium heat. Add Steak. Sprinkle with Flour and brown.
2. Add Onions, Pepper, and Garlic and cook until vegetables are softened.
3. Stir in Chili Powder and Cumin. Add Diced Tomatoes, Beef Broth, Potatoes, Corn, and Salt.
4. Bring to a boil, reduce heat, and simmer covered for 30 minutes, stirring occasionally.

GAME ON
This chili is a hearty and delicious Game Day option because it is a departure from a traditional chili recipe. When you serve it in our Bread Bowl (recipe found at the end of this section) made with frozen bread dough, you are sure to have a winner.

Sweet and Sour Stew

SERVES 6

- 1/2 C Flour
- 1 t Salt
- 1.5 lbs. Flank Steak, pounded to tenderize and chopped into 1" pieces
- 2 T Olive Oil
- 1 1/2 C Water
- 1/4 C Brown Sugar
- 3 T White Wine Vinegar
- 1/2 C Ketchup
- 1 T Salt
- 1 C Onion or 1/2 C Shallot, chopped
- 1 T Worcestershire Sauce
- 1 C Carrots, chopped
- 2 4 oz. cans Mushrooms, drained
- 2 C Potatoes, peeled and chopped
- 1/2 C Water
- 3 T Flour

1. Combine Flour and Salt in small bowl. Coat Flank Steak by rolling it in the Flour mixture. Heat Olive Oil in fry pan, add coated Flank Steak, and brown meat.
2. In stock pot, combine Water, Brown Sugar, Vinegar, Ketchup, Salt, Onion/Shallot, and Worcestershire Sauce.
3. Add browned meat and simmer for 45 minutes. Stir in Carrots, Mushrooms, and Potatoes and simmer for an additional 45 minutes.
4. Mix together 1/2 C Water and 3 T Flour mixture. Stir into soup to thicken.

98

Vichyssoise (vee-shee-SWAHZ) (Cold)

SERVES 6

- 2 T Unsalted Butter
- 1 C Green Onions, thinly sliced
- 2 C Potatoes, peeled and cubed
- 2 15 oz. cans or 4 C Chicken Broth
- 1 C Milk
- 1 1/2 t Salt
- 1/4 t Nutmeg
- 1 C Sour Cream/Plain Yogurt

1. Melt Butter over low heat in stock pot. Add Green Onions and sauté until very soft.
2. Add remaining ingredients, except Sour Cream/Plain Yogurt, and turn up heat to medium. Cover and bring to a boil. Cook until Potatoes are fork tender. (20-30 minutes)
3. Cool. Place in blender (in batches if necessary) and blend until smooth. Stir in Sour Cream/Plain Yogurt.
4. Let set 10 additional minutes. Top with additional sliced Green Onion, if desired, before serving.

WHAT IS VICHYSSOISE?
Vichyssoise is a French soup made from potatoes and onions. It is generally served chilled or at room temperature and has a lovely and light, creamy texture. Try serving with Flank Steak kebabs for a new twist on meat and potatoes!

White Bean and Ham Soup

SERVES 6

- 1 T Unsalted Butter
- 1/2 C Shallot or 1 C Onion, diced
- 1 C Celery, chopped
- 1 C Carrots, chopped
- 2 cloves Garlic, minced
- 2 15 oz. cans Northern/Cannelini Beans, undrained
- 1 C Ham, diced
- 1 15 oz. can or 2 C Chicken Broth
- 1 t Salt

1. Melt Unsalted Butter in stock pot over medium heat.
2. Add Shallot/Onion, Celery, Carrots, and Garlic and cook until softened.
3. Take one can of the Beans and mash them with a fork.
4. Stir in all Beans, Ham, Chicken Broth, and Salt into the stock pot.
5. Cover and simmer for 20 minutes. Let set 10 additional minutes before serving.

BREADS

We are huge fans of Frozen Bread Dough for its versatility and fresh baked bread taste. Try these breads as great accompaniments to your Soups, Salads, or various dishes.

Bread Bowls

SERVES 2 - 4

- 1 loaf Frozen Bread Dough
- 2 T Unsalted Butter, melted

1. Cut thawed Bread Dough into 4 pieces (or 2 pieces for larger bowls).
2. Roll chunks into balls. Place on a Parchment Paper covered jelly roll pan.
3. Cover with greased Plastic Wrap and allow to double in size (takes 2-4 hours).
4. Remove Plastic Wrap and bake at 350°F for 20 minutes.

FROZEN BREAD DOUGH QUICK THAW METHOD

These quick thaw methods save you a lot of time when making any of the dishes that use frozen bread dough!

OVEN: Preheat the oven to 325°F. Wrap a loaf of frozen bread dough in a sheet of parchment paper like a burrito and place seam side down in a loaf pan. Place in oven for approximately 12 minutes.

MICROWAVE: Spray a microwave safe loaf pan or mixing bowl with non-stick spray. Place frozen bread dough in pan. Cover with plastic wrap. Microwave for 15 seconds, uncover, and flip bread over. Re-cover and repeat until bread is thawed.

Breadsticks

SERVES 4 - 6

- 2 loaves Frozen Bread Dough
- 2 T Unsalted Butter, melted
- 1/2 T Garlic Powder
- 1/2 C Parmesan Cheese

1. Cut thawed Bread Dough into 8 pieces.
2. Roll chunks into long ropes. Place on Parchment Paper covered jelly roll pan.
3. Cover with greased Plastic Wrap and allow to double in size (takes 2-4 hours).
4. Baste with melted Butter. Sprinkle with Garlic Powder and Parmesan Cheese.
5. Bake at 350°F for 20 minutes.

102

Cheddar Chili Roll-Up Bread

SERVES 4 - 6

- 1 loaf Frozen Bread Dough, thawed
- 2/3 C Cheddar Cheese, shredded
- 2 T Parmesan Cheese
- 1 T Chili Powder

1. Gently stretch the dough into a 9" wide rectangle. Sprinkle with Cheeses and Chili Powder from above. Roll up, starting with one shorter end, and place in greased loaf pan seam side down.
2. Cover and place somewhere warm for a couple of hours to rise until it's an inch over the top of the pan.
3. Preheat oven to 350°F. Bake for 20-25 minutes or until golden brown.

Cheesy Ranch Roll-Up Bread

SERVES 4 - 6

- 1 loaf Frozen Bread Dough, thawed
- 1/4 C Ranch Dressing
- 1/4 C Mozzarella or Cheddar Cheese, shredded

1. Gently stretch the dough into a 9" wide rectangle. Spread with Ranch Dressing and sprinkle over top with Mozzarella Cheese. Roll up, starting with one shorter end, and place in greased loaf pan seam side down.
2. Cover and place somewhere warm for a couple of hours to rise until it's an inch over the top of the pan.
3. Preheat oven to 350°F. Bake for 20-25 minutes or until golden brown.

AGAIN...
FROZEN BREAD DOUGH QUICK THAW METHOD

These quick thaw methods save you a lot of time when making any of the dishes that use frozen bread dough!

OVEN: Preheat the oven to 325°F. Wrap a loaf of frozen bread dough in a sheet of parchment paper like a burrito and place seam side down in a loaf pan. Place in oven for approximately 12 minutes.

MICROWAVE: Spray a microwave safe loaf pan or mixing bowl with non-stick spray. Place frozen bread dough in pan. Cover with plastic wrap. Microwave for 15 seconds, uncover, and flip bread over. Re-cover and repeat until bread is thawed.

Cinnamon Raisin Roll-Up Bread

SERVES 4 - 6

- 1 loaf Frozen Bread Dough, thawed
- 1/4 C Sugar
- 1 t Cinnamon
- 2 T Unsalted Butter, melted
- 1/2 C Raisins

1. Gently stretch the dough into a 9" wide rectangle. Mix together Sugar, Cinnamon, and melted Butter. Spread over Bread Dough. Sprinkle with Raisins. Roll up, starting with one shorter end, and place in greased loaf pan seam side down.
2. Cover and place somewhere warm for a couple of hours to rise until it's an inch over the top of the pan.
3. Preheat oven to 350°F. Bake for 20-25 minutes or until golden brown.

ONE MORE TIME...
FROZEN BREAD DOUGH QUICK THAW METHOD

These quick thaw methods save you a lot of time when making any of the dishes that use frozen bread dough!

OVEN: Preheat the oven to 325°F. Wrap a loaf of frozen bread dough in a sheet of parchment paper like a burrito and place seam side down in a loaf pan. Place in oven for approximately 12 minutes.

MICROWAVE: Spray a microwave safe loaf pan or mixing bowl with non-stick spray. Place frozen bread dough in pan. Cover with plastic wrap. Microwave for 15 seconds, uncover, and flip bread over. Re-cover and repeat until bread is thawed.

Garlic Parmesan Roll-Up Bread SK

SERVES 4 - 6

- 1 loaf Frozen Bread Dough, thawed
- 2 T Olive Oil
- 1 clove Garlic, minced
- 1/2 C Parmesan Cheese

1. Gently stretch the dough into a 9" wide rectangle. Mix together Olive Oil and Garlic and spread over Bread Dough. Sprinkle Parmesan on top. Roll up, starting with one shorter end, and place in greased loaf pan seam side down.
2. Cover and place somewhere warm for a couple of hours to rise until it's an inch over the top of the pan.
3. Preheat oven to 350°F. Bake for 20-25 minutes or until golden brown.

106

Grilled Flat Bread

SERVES 4 - 6

- 1 loaf Frozen Bread Dough, thawed
- 2 T Olive Oil
- 1/4 t Garlic Powder (or to taste)

1. Cut thawed Bread Dough into four even pieces. Roll out each piece into a round flat disk (about 5 - 6 inches in diameter).
2. Brush Olive Oil evenly on both sides and sprinkle with Garlic Powder.
3. Place directly on the rack of a preheated grill (medium) for about 5 minutes and then flip for another 5 minutes.

GRILLED BREAD?
Although this is an unconventional recipe, the results are outstanding. We love this bread's crisp outside and chewy inside! Experiment with different spices and flavorings, just make sure to roll them deep into the bread dough before grilling. Try using this bread as a "plate" for salads.

Pastas and Pizzas

veggie pizza

peanut noodles

tomato artichoke pasta with shrimp

margherita pizza

chicken bbq pizza

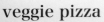

stovetop mac and cheese

PASTAS

These Pastas are our "go to" recipes for busy weekday dinners. We always salt our pasta water to make our pasta much more flavorful. A good rule of thumb is 1/2 tablespoon of salt per quart of water.

Baked Penne

SERVES 8

- 1 lb. Penne Pasta
- 1 lb. Ground Beef/Ground Breakfast Sausage
- 2 T Italian Seasoning
- 1 Shallot or 1/2 Onion, diced
- 2 cloves Garlic, minced
- 1 Bell Pepper, finely chopped

- 1 4 oz. can Mushrooms
- 2 15 oz. can Diced Tomatoes
- 1 15 oz. can Tomato Sauce
- 1/4 C Fresh Basil, minced
- 2 T Brown Sugar
- 2 C Mozzarella Cheese
- 1/2 C Parmesan Cheese

1. Preheat oven to 350°F. Begin cooking Pasta according to package directions.
2. In a large fry pan or stock pot, brown meat and drain grease. Add Italian Seasoning, Shallot/Onion, Garlic, and Bell Pepper and cook over medium heat until vegetables are tender.
3. Mix in Mushrooms, Diced Tomatoes, Tomato Sauce, Basil, and Sugar. Combine with cooked Penne and pour into a 9" x 13" baking dish. Top with Cheeses.
4. Bake for 30 minutes or until Cheeses begin to brown.

MAKE, THEN BAKE
This dish is perfect for serving when another family comes to dinner. We make it a few hours ahead and refrigerate. Then just before they come, we stick it in the oven. It is cheesy and delicious and very child friendly. Best of all, we are able to enjoy our guests!

110

Lemon Dill Seafood Pasta

SERVES 4 - 6

- 6 oz. - 1/2 pound Pasta of your choice
- 2 T Unsalted Butter
- 3 cloves Garlic, minced
- 2 T Flour
- 1 1/2 C Milk
- 1/2 C Sour Cream/Plain Yogurt
- 1/4 C Parmesan Cheese
- 1/2 T Salt
- 1/4 t Pepper

- 1/8 t Nutmeg (optional)
- 12 oz. - 1 lb. Shrimp, raw, peeled, de-veined, de-tailed, and thawed
- 1 6 oz. pkg. Crab Meat, imitation (chopped) or canned lump (drained)
- 1/4 C Green Onion, thinly sliced
- 1 t Dill Weed
- 2 T Lemon Juice

1. Begin cooking Pasta according to package directions.
2. In saucepan over medium heat, melt Butter. Mix in Garlic and cook until softened. Do not let Garlic brown.
3. Add Flour and whisk together, creating a roux. Let roux cook for about a minute.
4. Slowly whisk in Milk, 1/2 C at a time, until smooth. Cook until thickened.
5. Once mixture is thickened and bubbling, mix in Sour Cream, Parmesan, Salt, Pepper, and Nutmeg. Allow mixture to heat through.
6. Add Shrimp and Crab to sauce, continuing to cook over medium heat until Shrimp are pink and done. Stir in Green Onion, Dill, and Lemon Juice. Toss with Pasta.

THICK AND CREAMY WITHOUT THE CREAM

In our Alfredo based sauces we use a "roux" which is basically a thickening agent made up of equal parts flour and fat. We generally use butter. Roux are fairly simple, however it is important to whisk the sauce smooth, and make sure the flour is completely incorporated, to avoid lumps.

Mediterranean Pasta SK

SERVES 4 - 6

- 6 oz. - 1/2 pound Pasta of your choice
- 1/4 C Olive Oil
- 1 clove Garlic, minced
- 1/4 C Shallot or 1/2 C Onion, diced
- 1/2 C Roasted Red Peppers, diced
- 1/4 C Black Olives, sliced
- 2 C Frozen Spinach, thawed
- 1/2 t Salt
- 1/4 t Pepper
- 1 T Lemon Juice
- 3/4 C Feta Cheese
- 1/2 C Pine Nuts

1. Begin cooking Pasta according to package directions.
2. Add 2 T of Olive Oil to a fry pan over medium heat. Cook Garlic and Shallot or Onion until softened. Add Peppers, Olives, Spinach, Salt, and Pepper and sauté until heated through.
3. Toss with Pasta, remaining Olive Oil, Lemon Juice, Feta Cheese, and Pine Nuts.
4. Try topped with grilled Chicken, grilled Flank Steak, or sauteed or grilled Shrimp.

112

Pasta Carbonara

SERVES 4 - 6

- 6 oz. - 1/2 pound Pasta of your choice
- 1 t Salt
- 2 cloves Garlic, peeled
- 3 slices Bacon, cut into 1/4 inch pieces
- 3/4 C Milk
- 3 Eggs, yolks only
- 1/2 C Parmesan Cheese
- 1 t Salt
- 3/4 C Frozen Peas, thawed

1. Bring a stock pot of water with 2 whole peeled cloves of Garlic and 1 t Salt to a boil. Add Pasta of choice and cook according to package ingredients.
2. In a fry pan, cook Bacon until crispy. Drain excess grease off, turn heat to low and whisk in Milk, Egg Yolks, Parmesan Cheese, and Salt. Whisk continuously until mixture begins to thicken.
3. When Pasta is done, remove Garlic, drain Pasta into a colander and set aside. Cut off the ends of Garlic and mash with the side of a large knife.
4. Toss sauce with mashed Garlic, Pasta, and Peas. Serve with extra Parmesan Cheese. Try topped with grilled Chicken, grilled Flank Steak, sauteed or grilled Shrimp, or Crab Meat.

SEPARATING EGG YOLKS

The best way to separate out your egg yolks from the egg whites is to crack the eggs in half and pour the egg yolk from one shell half to the other allowing the egg whites to fall out of the shell. Depending on if you are using the whites or the yolks, capture the egg whites in a bowl as they escape.

Pasta Primavera

SERVES 4 - 6

- 6 oz. - 1/2 pound Pasta of your choice
- 2 T Unsalted Butter
- 1/4 C Shallot or 1/2 C Onion, thinly sliced
- 1 Bell Pepper, finely diced
- 1 Carrot, peeled and finely diced
- 3 cloves Garlic, minced
- 2 T Flour
- 1 1/2 C Milk
- 1/2 C Sour Cream/Plain Yogurt
- 1/4 C Parmesan Cheese
- 1/2 T Salt
- 1/4 t Pepper
- 1/8 t Nutmeg (optional)
- 2 C Frozen Broccoli
- 1 T Italian Seasoning
- 12 oz. - 1 lb. Shrimp, raw, peeled, de-veined, and de-tailed (optional)

1. Begin cooking Pasta according to package directions.
2. In saucepan over medium heat, melt Butter. Mix in Garlic, Shallot/Onions, Bell Pepper, and Carrots and cook until softened. Do not let Garlic brown.
3. Add Flour and whisk together creating a roux. Let roux cook for about a minute.
4. Slowly whisk in Milk and cook until thickened.
5. Once mixture is thickened and bubbling, mix in Sour Cream, Parmesan, Salt, Pepper, Nutmeg, Frozen Broccoli, and Italian Seasoning (if adding Shrimp, add it here). Allow mixture to heat through (or until Shrimp are pink).
6. Toss with Sauce and Pasta. If you don't like Shrimp, try topping Pasta with grilled Chicken, grilled Flank Steak, or Crab Meat.

114

Peanut Noodles SK

SERVES 8

- 1 lb. Thin Pasta

PEANUT SAUCE
- 3/4 C Peanut Butter
- 1/3 C Soy Sauce
- 1/4 C Honey
- 1 1/2 T Lemon Juice
- 1 T Ginger
- 1 clove Garlic, minced
- 1/4 t Tabasco/Hot Sauce (or to taste)

- 1/2 C Warm Water
- 1/2 C Milk
- 3 Green Onions, sliced
- 1/2 Bell Pepper, cut into thin strips
- 1/2 English Cucumber, diced

1. Cook Pasta according to its package directions.
2. In a mixing bowl, combine PEANUT SAUCE ingredients. Add warm Water and Milk. Place cooked Pasta in a serving bowl and pour PEANUT SAUCE over top. Toss to coat.
3. Sprinkle Green Onions, Bell Pepper, and Cucumber over Pasta. Serve at room temperature.
4. Try topped with grilled Chicken, grilled Flank Steak, or grilled Shrimp.

PEANUT SAUCE USES
Try making this Peanut Sauce recipe and then mix only half of the Peanut Sauce with half of the water, Milk, Pasta, etc. This serves 4. Then, use the remainder of the Peanut Sauce as a marinade (see Meats) or on top of a Thai Peanut Pizza. This sauce is exceptional and versatile.

Pink Alfredo Pasta

SERVES 4 - 6

- 6 oz. - 1/2 pound Pasta of your choice
- 2 T Unsalted Butter
- 3 cloves Garlic, minced
- 2 T Flour
- 1 1/2 C Milk
- 1/2 C Sour Cream/Plain Yogurt
- 1/4 C Parmesan Cheese
- 1/2 T Salt
- 1/4 t Pepper
- 1/8 t Nutmeg (optional)
- 1 15 oz. Diced Tomatoes (with liquid)
- 1/4 t Crushed Red Pepper
- 2 T Olive Oil
- 12 oz. - 1 lb. Shrimp, raw, peeled, de-veined, and de-tailed (optional)

1. Begin cooking Pasta according to package directions.
2. In saucepan over medium heat, melt Butter. Mix in Garlic and cook until softened. Do not let Garlic brown.
3. Add Flour and whisk together creating a roux. Let roux cook for about a minute.
4. Slowly whisk in Milk and cook until thickened.
5. Once mixture is thickened and bubbling, mix in Sour Cream, Parmesan, Salt, Pepper, Diced Tomatoes, Crushed Red Pepper, and Olive Oil (if adding Shrimp, add it here). Allow mixture to heat through (or until Shrimp are pink).
6. Toss with Sauce and Pasta. If you don't like Shrimp, try topping Pasta with grilled Chicken, grilled Flank Steak, or Crab Meat.

116

Quick Marinara and Meatballs SK

SERVES 4 - 6

- 6 oz. - 1/2 pound Pasta of your choice
- 1 T Olive Oil
- 1/4 C Shallot or 1/2 C Onion, diced
- 2 cloves of Garlic, minced
- 1/2 Bell Pepper (optional)
- 1/4 C Tomato Paste
- 2 15 oz. cans Diced Tomatoes
- 1 15 oz. can or 2 C Beef Broth
- 2 T Sugar
- 1/4 C Fresh Basil, chopped
- 2 T Italian Seasonings
- 1 T Anise Seed/Fennel Seed (optional)

MEATBALLS
- 1 lb. Ground Beef
- 1/2 C Plain Bread Crumbs
- 1 T Italian Seasonings
- 2 Eggs, lightly beaten
- 2 T Dried Minced Onions
- 1 t Salt
- 1/4 t Pepper

1. Begin cooking Pasta according to package directions.
2. In a stock pot over medium heat, add Olive Oil. Let it get warm and then add Shallot or Onion, Garlic, and Bell Pepper and cook until vegetables soften.
3. Add Tomato Paste and sauté for a couple of minutes to reduce its bitterness.
4. Add remaining ingredients (make sure to crush the Anise or Fennel seed in your hand before adding) and bring to a boil.
5. Mix MEATBALLS ingredients with your hands. Roll into 2 inch balls and add to sauce. Allow to cook in boiling sauce for 30 minutes or until MEATBALLS cooked through.

TOSS IT IN
My grandmother and mother first taught me the concept of "use what you have" and this sauce is a perfect example. When this sauce gets to a rolling boil, we throw in not only the Meatballs, but also pieces of chicken, and will even crack in eggs for a meatless dish. Boil for 30 minutes or until chicken is cooked or eggs are hard-boiled.

Southwest Pasta

SERVES 4 - 6

- 6 oz. - 1/2 pound Pasta of your choice
- 2 oz. Cream Cheese
- 1 C Salsa
- 1 C Cheddar Cheese, shredded
- 2 t Cumin
- 1 T Chili Powder
- 1 15 oz. can Kidney Beans, rinsed and drained
- 1 15 oz. can Corn, drained

1. Start cooking Pasta according to package directions.
2. Over medium heat in a saucepan, stir together Cream Cheese, Salsa, Cheese, Cumin, and Chili Powder until smooth.
3. Stir in remaining ingredients and heat through. Toss with Pasta and serve. Try topped with grilled Chicken, grilled Flank Steak, Ground Breakfast Sausage (browned and drained), or Ground Beef (browned and drained).

SPICY TOLERANCE
All of these recipes will taste differently based on the ingredients that you choose. This recipe, for instance, can go from very mild to super spicy based on what type of salsa. If it is still not spicy enough for you, add some Tabasco to really pack in the heat.

118

"Stocked" Alfredo Pasta

SERVES 4 - 6

- 6 oz. - 1/2 pound Pasta of your choice
- 2 T Unsalted Butter
- 3 cloves Garlic, minced
- 2 T Flour
- 1 1/2 C Milk
- 1/2 C Sour Cream/Plain Yogurt

- 1/4 C Parmesan Cheese
- 1/2 T Salt
- 1/4 t Pepper
- 1/8 t Nutmeg (optional)
- 12 oz. - 1 lb. Shrimp, raw, peeled, deveined, and de-tailed (optional)

1. Begin cooking Pasta according to package directions.
2. In saucepan over medium heat, melt Butter. Mix in Garlic and cook until softened. Do not let Garlic brown.
3. Add Flour and whisk together creating a roux. Let roux cook for about a minute.
4. Slowly whisk in Milk, 1/2 C at a time, until smooth. Cook until thickened.
5. Once mixture is thickened and bubbling, mix in Sour Cream, Parmesan, Salt, Pepper, and Nutmeg (if adding Shrimp, add it here). Allow mixture to heat through (or until Shrimp are pink).
6. Toss with Sauce and Pasta. If you don't like Shrimp, try topping Pasta with grilled Chicken, grilled Flank Steak, or Crab Meat.

ALFREDO PIZZA SAUCE
This Alfredo Sauce also makes an amazing pizza sauce. We like to spread it over pizza dough and top with mozzarella, shrimp, broccoli, or any "Stocked" toppings.

Stove Top Mac and Cheese SK

SERVES 4 - 6

- 4 C Egg Noodles or 6 oz. Penne Pasta
- 1 Egg
- 3/4 C Sour Cream/Plain Yogurt
- 1 T Unsalted Butter
- 1/4 C Milk
- 1t Salt
- Pepper (to taste)
- 1 1/2 C Cheddar Cheese, shredded

1. Cook Pasta according to package directions. After cooking and draining the Pasta, return to saucepan. Heat on low, add Butter, and stir until melted.
2. In a bowl whisk together Egg, Sour Cream/Yogurt, Milk, Salt, and Pepper. Add to pot with Cheese.
3. Continue to cook over low heat, stirring until smooth.
4. Try topped with Ham or our Sloppy Joe recipe.

A MORE CHILD FRIENDLY OPTION
This recipe tastes different (and as far as we are concerned, much better) than the pre-packaged boxes. Your children might prefer a mild cheddar cheese. Also, try only using 3/4 C cheddar and 3/4 C mozzarella to give it an even smoother taste.

Stroganoff

SERVES 4 - 6

- 4 C Egg Noodles or 6 oz. Penne Pasta
- 1 1/2 T Unsalted Butter
- 1/4 C Shallots or 1/2 C Onions, thinly sliced
- 1 4 oz. can Mushrooms
- 1 1/2 T Flour
- 1/4 t Garlic Powder
- 1 t Salt
- 1/8 t Pepper
- 1 C Beef Broth
- 1/2 T Worcestershire Sauce
- 1/2 t Dill Weed
- 1/2 C Sour Cream/Plain Yogurt

1. Start cooking Pasta according to package directions.
2. In fry pan, melt Butter over medium heat.
3. Add Shallots/Onions and Mushrooms and saute for about 5 - 6 minutes.
4. Stir in Flour, Garlic Powder, Salt, and Pepper and let cook 2 - 3 minutes. Whisk in Beef Broth gradually and bring to a boil, stirring occasionally until thickened, approximately 8 minutes. Reduce heat and simmer for 5 - 6 more minutes.
5. Stir in Worcestershire Sauce, Dill Weed, and Sour Cream/Plain Yogurt.
6. Toss with Pasta and serve. Try topped with Grilled Flank Steak, Ground Beef (browned and drained) or our baked Meatball recipe.

Tomato Artichoke Pasta SK

SERVES 4 - 6

- 6 oz. - 1/2 pound Pasta of your choice
- 1/4 C Olive Oil
- 2 cloves of Garlic, minced
- 1 C Marinated Artichoke Hearts, drained
- 1 C Tomato, diced or 1 15 oz. can Diced Tomatoes
- 1/4 C Fresh Basil, chopped
- 1 T Italian Seasonings
- 1/2 t Salt (or to taste)
- Pepper (to taste)
- 12 oz. - 1 lb. Shrimp, raw, peeled, de-veined, and de-tailed (optional)

1. Start cooking Pasta according to package directions.
2. In a fry pan over medium heat, add 2 T Olive Oil and Garlic. Allow Garlic to soften but not burn.
3. Add remaining ingredients (including thawed Shrimp if desired) and sauté for 5 minutes.
4. Toss with Pasta and remaining Olive Oil and serve with Parmesan Cheese. If you don't like Shrimp, try topping Pasta with grilled Chicken, grilled Flank Steak, or Crab Meat.

"ALWAYS BE A GUEST AT YOUR OWN PARTY"
We are big proponents of enjoying our get-togethers and dinner parties just as much as our guests. This recipe is perfect for that because it is fast, easy, and impressive. Best of all you aren't stuck in the kitchen all night! Serve with our Italian Vinaigrette Salad and freshly baked Bread, and ENJOY!

122

Breadsticks

SERVES 6

- 2 loaves Frozen Bread Dough
- 2 T Unsalted Butter, melted
- 1/2 T Garlic Powder
- 1/2 C Parmesan Cheese

1. Preheat oven to 350°F.
2. Cut thawed Bread Dough into 8 pieces.
3. Roll chunks into long ropes. Place on Parchment Paper covered jelly roll pan.
4. Cover with greased Plastic Wrap and allow to double in size (takes 2-4 hours).
5. Baste with melted Butter. Sprinkle with Garlic Powder and Parmesan Cheese.
6. Bake for 20 minutes.

> **FROZEN BREAD DOUGH QUICK THAW METHOD**
>
> These quick thaw methods save you a lot of time when making any of the dishes that use frozen bread dough!
>
> OVEN: Preheat the oven to 325°F. Wrap a loaf of frozen bread dough in a sheet of parchment paper like a burrito and place seam side down in a loaf pan. Place in oven for approximately 12 minutes.
>
> MICROWAVE: Spray a microwave safe loaf pan or mixing bowl with non-stick spray. Place frozen bread dough in pan. Cover with plastic wrap. Microwave for 15 seconds, uncover, and flip bread over. Re-cover and repeat until bread is thawed.

PIZZAS

These pizzas not only taste great, but they are a fun activity to do as a family. We love having friends over for "make your own pizza" night!

Pizza Crust

SERVES 4

- 1 loaf Frozen Bread Dough, thawed (see tip on next page)
- 2 T Olive Oil

1. Preheat oven to 400°F. Spread out Bread Dough over greased, deep dish pizza pan or jelly roll pan and drizzle Olive Oil over dough, covering crust.
2. Build your own pizza with our Pizza Sauce recipe and suggested Toppings. This crust also works great for any of our Specialty Pizzas in this section.
3. Bake for 10 - 15 minutes or until crust is golden brown and bottom is crispy.

THE PIZZA DOUGH GRIP
Don't be delicate with this dough. Show it who's boss! We cover our hands with olive oil, mold the dough into a ball and then grip it like a steering wheel with the palms of our hands facing away and our fingers tucked into the back side of the dough. We grip it and turn it until it starts to release. Keep turning it until it becomes shaped more like a crust, lay it on the pan, and push it to the desired thickness and shape.

Pizza Crust (Individual)

SERVES 4

- 1 loaf Frozen Bread Dough, thawed
- 2 T Olive Oil

1. Cut thawed Bread Dough into 4 individual balls.
2. Preheat oven to 400°F. Pull apart each of the four balls of dough into 6" or 7" diameter rounds. Lay onto a greased pizza pan or jelly roll pan and drizzle Olive Oil over dough, covering crust.
3. Build your own pizza with our Pizza Sauce recipe and suggested Toppings. This crust also works great for any of our Specialty Pizzas in this section.
4. Bake for 10 - 15 minutes or until crust is golden brown and bottom is crispy.

DON'T FORGET...
FROZEN BREAD DOUGH QUICK THAW METHOD

These quick thaw methods save you a lot of time when making any of the dishes that use frozen bread dough!

OVEN: Preheat the oven to 325°F. Wrap a loaf of frozen bread dough in a sheet of parchment paper like a burrito and place seam side down in a loaf pan. Place in oven for approximately 12 minutes.

MICROWAVE: Spray a microwave safe loaf pan or mixing bowl with non-stick spray. Place frozen bread dough in pan. Cover with plastic wrap. Microwave for 15 seconds, uncover, and flip bread over. Re-cover and repeat until bread is thawed.

Pita Pizza Crust

SERVES 4

- 4 Pita Bread

1. Preheat oven to 400°F. On a Parchment Paper covered jelly roll pan, lay out Pita Bread.
2. Build your own pizza with our Pizza Sauce recipe and suggested Toppings. This crust also works great for any of our Specialty Pizzas in this section.
3. Bake for 10 - 12 minutes.

PIZZA PARTY
The Individual Pizza Crust and Pita Pizza Crust are fun for both children and adults. We like to set out sauce and toppings and then let everyone put his or her own pizza concoction together. It's a great activity and everyone has a meal to enjoy.

Pizza Sauce SK

- 1 15 oz. can Tomato Sauce
- 1/4 C Tomato Paste
- 1/4 t Garlic Powder
- 2 T Italian Seasoning
- 3 T Brown Sugar

1. Mix ingredients together and use immediately or refrigerate for later use. Making at least an hour ahead helps flavors to meld.

Pizza Toppings

- Mozzarella Cheese
- Cheddar Cheese
- Feta Cheese
- Bleu/Gorgonzola Cheese
- Parmesan Cheese
- Ham
- Ground Breakfast Sausage, cooked and drained
- Ground Beef, cooked and drained
- Bacon, cooked
- Chicken, cooked and cubed
- Shrimp, cooked
- Mushrooms
- Spinach
- Bell Pepper
- Shallot/Onions
- Marinated Artichoke Hearts
- Pineapple
- Roasted Red Peppers
- Black Olives
- Green/Calamata Olives
- Tomatoes

Chicken BBQ Pizza

SERVES 4

- 1 C Barbecue Sauce
- 1 T Honey (optional)
- 1/4 lb. Boneless Skinless Chicken, cooked and cubed
- 3 slices Bacon, cooked and chopped (optional)
- 1 1/2 C Mozzarella or Cheddar Cheese
- 1/2 Bell Pepper, thinly sliced
- 1/4 C Shallot/Onion, diced

1. Preheat oven to 400°F.
2. Choose Frozen Bread Dough Pizza Crust or Pita Pizza Crust from beginning of section.
3. Mix together Barbecue Sauce and Honey. Spread sauce over crust(s).
4. Top with remaining ingredients and bake according to crust directions.

128

Margherita Pizza

SERVES 4

- 1 Tomato, very thinly sliced
- 2 T Olive Oil
- 2 cloves Garlic, minced
- 1/2 t Salt
- 1/4 t Pepper
- 1 C Mozzarella Cheese
- 1/2 C Fresh Basil
- 1/2 C Parmesan Cheese

1. Preheat oven to 400°F.
2. Choose Frozen Bread Dough Pizza Crust or Pita Pizza Crust from beginning of section.
3. Lay thinly sliced Tomatoes out over crust(s). Mix Oil and Garlic together. Spread Oil and Garlic evenly over Tomatoes. Sprinkle with Salt and Pepper.
4. Top with Mozzarella Cheese, then whole Basil leaves, and then Parmesan Cheese.
5. Bake according to crust directions.

Pesto Spinach Pizza SK

SERVES 4

PESTO SAUCE
- 1 C Fresh Basil
- 3 T Pine Nuts
- 1/4 C Parmesan Cheese
- 2 cloves Garlic, peeled
- 1/4 C Olive Oil
- 1/2 t Salt
- 1/4 t Pepper

- 1 C Frozen Spinach, thawed and squeezed dry
- 1 C Mozzarella Cheese
- 1/2 C Feta or Parmesan Cheese
- 1 Roasted Red Pepper, chopped (optional)
- 1 Shallot or Onion, thinly sliced

1. Preheat oven to 400°F.
2. Choose Frozen Bread Dough Pizza Crust or Pita Pizza Crust from beginning of section.
3. Place Basil, Pine Nuts, Parmesan, Garlic, Olive Oil, Salt, and Pepper in a Food Processor/Blender and blend until smooth. Spread this PESTO SAUCE over crust(s).
4. Top with Spinach, then Feta, then Roasted Red Pepper, and then Shallot/Onion.
5. Bake according to crust directions.

PESTO SAUCE
Try this Pesto Sauce as a delicious pasta sauce by adding 1/2 C of chicken broth. It is also delicious as a dipping sauce for our Breadsticks recipe!

130

Thai Peanut Pizza

SERVES 4

PEANUT SAUCE
- 1/3 C Peanut Butter
- 2 T Soy Sauce
- 2 T Honey
- 2 t Lemon Juice
- 1 T Ginger
- 1 Garlic, minced
- 1/4 t Tabasco/Hot Sauce (or to taste)

- 1/4 lb. Boneless Skinless Chicken, cooked and thinly sliced (optional)
- 1 Carrot, thinly sliced with a peeler
- 1 1/2 C Mozzarella Cheese
- 2 Green Onions, thinly sliced

1. Preheat oven to 400°F.
2. Choose Frozen Bread Dough Pizza Crust or Pita Pizza Crust from beginning of section.
3. In a mixing bowl, combine Peanut Butter, Soy Sauce, Honey, Lemon Juice, Ginger and Garlic. Spread this PEANUT SAUCE over crust(s).
4. Top with Chicken and Carrots, then Mozzarella Cheese, and then Green Onions.
5. Bake according to crust directions.

Veggie Pizza

SERVES 4

- 1 8 oz. pkg. Cream Cheese, softened
- 1 C Ranch Dressing
- 1 1/2 C Cheddar or Mozzarella Cheese
- 1 C Frozen Broccoli, thawed, drained, and finely chopped
- 1 4 oz. can Mushrooms, well drained and sliced or chopped
- 1/4 C Black Olives, well drained and sliced or chopped

1. Preheat oven to 400°F.
2. Choose Frozen Bread Dough Pizza Crust or Pita Pizza Crust from beginning of section.
3. Spread Cream Cheese evenly over crust(s). Top evenly with Ranch Dressing.
4. Top with Cheese and then remaining ingredients. Bake according to crust directions.

SOFTENING CREAM CHEESE OR BUTTER
The best way to soften items like Cream Cheese or Butter is to let it set out until it naturally becomes softened. We suggest only using your microwave if you have a "soften" setting on it. Otherwise you can wind up with a soupy recipe!

NOTES

Meat, Chicken, and Seafood

MARINADES

Asian Marinade (p.135)
Greek Marinade (p.135)
Honey Lime Marinade (p.135)
Italian Marinade (p.135)
Java Marinade (p.136)
Lemon Pepper Marinade (p.136)
Moroccan Marinade (p.136)
Thai Peanut Marinade (p.136)

CHICKEN

Apricot Chicken (p.138)
Bleu Cheese and Pear Chicken (p.138)
Chicken Cordon Bleu with Rice (p.139)
Chicken Enchiladas (p.140)
Chicken Fajitas (p.141)
Chicken Pot Pie (p.142)
Chicken Saltimbocca (p.143)
Chicken Satay (p.144)
Chicken Strips (p.145)
Feta Chicken (p.146)
Ginger Broccoli Stir-Fry (p.147)
Mexican Chicken (p.147)
Nutty Chicken (p.148)
Sweet and Sour Stir-Fry (p.149)
Southwest Chicken and Rice (p.150)

FLANK STEAK

Black and Bleu Roll-Up (p.152)
Braised Provencal Steak (p.153)
Greek Roll-Up (p.154)
Jerk Rubbed Steak (p.155)
Moroccan Roll-Up (p.156)

Pepper & Fennel Rubbed Steak (p.157)
Pepper Steak (p.158)
Pesto Roll-Up (p.159)
Steak Fajitas (p.160)
Steak and Potato Shish Kebab (p.161)
Steak Wellington (p.162)

GROUND BEEF

Beef Enchiladas (p.163)
Beef Nachos (p.164)
Greek Burger (p.165)
Italian Burger (p.166)
Meatballs (p.167)
Meatloaf (p.168)
Sloppy Joes (p.169)
Southwest Burger (p.170)
Taco Meat (p.171)

SEAFOOD

Crab Cakes (p.173)
Crab Enchiladas (p.174)
Crab Noodle Casserole (p.175)
Lemon Pepper Shrimp (p.176)
Mock Shrimp Ceviche (p.177)
Moo Shoo Shrimp Stir Fry (p.178)
Pancake Batter Fried Shrimp (p.179)
Seafood Nachos (p.180)
Shrimp Cocktail (p.180)
Shrimp Fajitas (p.181)
Shrimp Pineapple Shish Kebabs (p.182)
Shrimp Scampi (p.182)

chicken saltimbocca

chicken strips

greek burgers

black and bleu roll-up

crab enchiladas

"mock" shrimp ceviche

MARINADES

These marinades can be used for either Flank Steak, Chicken, Shrimp, or fresh vegetables. Make sure to not to cross contaminate meats and/or vegetables and cook all meat and seafood dishes thoroughly. Consuming raw or undercooked meats or seafood may increase your risk of foodborne illness.

Asian Marinade

- 1/3 C Olive Oil
- 2 cloves Garlic, minced
- 2 T White Wine Vinegar
- 1/3 C Soy Sauce
- 1/4 C Honey
- 1/2 t Pepper
- 1/8 t Red Pepper Flakes

Greek Marinade

- 1/4 C Olive Oil
- 1/4 C Lemon Juice
- 1 T Lemon Zest (optional)
- 1 T Italian Seasoning
- 3 cloves Garlic, minced
- 1 T Dried Minced Onions
- 1 t Salt
- 1/4 t Pepper

Honey Lime Marinade

- 1/4 C Honey
- 2 T Vegetable Oil
- 1/4 C Lime Juice
- 1/2 t Salt
- 1/2 t Tabasco/Hot Sauce (or to taste)

Italian Marinade

- 2 T Extra Virgin Olive Oil
- 1/3 C Red Wine Vinegar
- 1 t Salt
- 1 t Sugar
- 1 T Italian Seasonings
- 1 clove Garlic, minced
- 1 T Dijon Mustard
- 1 t Dried Minced Onions

1. Mix all of the ingredients in a gallon size Resealable Storage Bag and shake, and then add meat or vegetables, and let marinade 2 - 24 hours.
2. Cook according to specific Flank Steak, Chicken, or Shrimp section directions.

Java Marinade

- 3 T Worcestershire sauce
- 1/2 C Coffee, strongly brewed and cooled
- 1/4 C Vegetable Oil
- 3 T Balsamic Vinegar
- 3 T Brown Sugar
- 2 t Salt
- 1/2 t Pepper
- 1 clove Garlic, minced
- 1 T Ginger

Lemon Pepper Marinade

- 1/2 C Lemon Juice
- 1/4 C Dijon Mustard
- 1 T Olive Oil
- 1 T Sugar
- 1 T Pepper
- 1 t Salt

Moroccan Marinade

- 1/2 C Olive Oil
- 2 t Ground Cumin
- 2 T Ginger
- 1 t Ground Cinnamon
- 1/4 C Lemon Juice
- 1 T Dried Minced Onions
- 1/2 t Salt
- 1/4 t Pepper

Thai Peanut Marinade

- 3/4 C Peanut Butter
- 1/3 C Soy Sauce
- 1/4 C Honey
- 1 1/2 T Lemon Juice
- 1 T Ginger
- 1 clove Garlic, minced
- 1/4 t Tabasco/Hot Sauce (or to taste)

1. Mix all of the ingredients in a gallon size Resealable Storage Bag and shake, and then add meat or vegetables, and let marinade 2 - 24 hours.
2. Cook according to specific Flank Steak, Chicken, or Shrimp section directions.

CHICKEN

Cooked chicken quickly makes a salad, pasta, or rice dish a complete meal. Here are a few ways to get the job done.

Poach:
1. In a stock pot place 4 Chicken Breasts, 2 cloves of Garlic, and 10 Peppercorns (optional).
2. Cover with 1 15 oz. can or 2 C Chicken Broth and, over medium high heat, bring to a boil. Reduce heat and simmer for 20 minutes. Remove Garlic and Pepper before using Chicken.

Pan-Fry:
1. Heat your fry pan to medium heat. Drizzle about a tablespoon of Olive Oil or Butter over the skillet for four Chicken Breasts or six Chicken Thighs.
2. Cook until white on one side and then turn and cook the other side until white. Lower the heat to medium low, cover, and let cook for about 5 more minutes or until cooked through. To cook faster, cut into strips or chunks before frying.

Bake:
1. Preheat the oven to 425°F. Lay out a large piece of Parchment Paper.
2. Place four Chicken Breasts or six Chicken Thighs on paper and sprinkle with Grill Seasonings or Salt and Pepper.
3. Wrap Chicken up in Parchment Paper like a burrito. Be sure to not wrap too tightly so that there is room for steam.
4. Place seam side down in an 8" square baking dish. Bake for 25 - 30 minutes. If using frozen Chicken Breasts, bake for 40 to 45 minutes or until cooked through.

138

Apricot Chicken SK

SERVES 4

- 1 lb. Boneless Skinless Chicken
- 1/2 t Salt
- 1/2 t Pepper
- 1 T Vegetable Oil

- 1 Shallot or 1/2 Onion, thinly sliced
- 1 15 oz. can Diced Tomatoes
- 1 C Apricot Preserves

1. Salt and Pepper both sides of Chicken.
2. In a fry pan, add Oil and sauté Shallots/Onions over medium heat.
3. Add Chicken. Top with Diced Tomatoes, and Apricot Preserves and sauté until Chicken is done, approximately 20 minutes.

Bleu Cheese and Pear Chicken

SERVES 4

- 1 lb. Boneless Skinless Chicken
- 1 t Salt
- 1 t Herbes De Provence
- 1 C Bleu/Gorgonzola Cheese

- 1 15 oz. can Pears, drained and chopped
- 1/4 C Balsamic Vinegar
- 2 T Olive Oil

1. Preheat oven to 375°F. Spray an 8" square baking dish with Non-Stick Spray.
2. Lay Chicken in baking dish and sprinkle with Salt and Herbes de Provence.
3. Sprinkle tops of Chicken with Bleu Cheese and then Pears. Whisk together Balsamic Vinegar and Olive Oil and drizzle over tops of Pears.
4. Cover with Aluminum Foil and bake for 35 to 40 minutes or until Chicken is fully cooked. If cooking frozen Chicken, bake for an additional 15 minutes or until cooked through.

Chicken Cordon Bleu with Rice SK

SERVES 4

- 3 T Dijon Mustard
- 1 C Rice, uncooked
- 1 15 oz. can or 2 C Chicken Broth
- 1/2 C Water
- 1 C Frozen Broccoli or Peas
- 1 lb. Boneless, Skinless Chicken
- 4 - 6 slices Ham (thin)
- 1 C Mozzarella Cheese
- 1/4 C Parmesan Cheese

1. Preheat the oven to 375°F.
2. Combine Mustard, Rice, Chicken Broth, Water, and Broccoli and spread on the bottom of a greased 9"x13" baking dish. Top with Chicken and cover Chicken with Ham and then Cheeses.
3. Cover pan with Aluminum Foil and bake for 40-45 minutes or until Chicken and Rice are completely cooked.

QUICK PREP
Have time to bake, but no time to prepare? This family friendly dish allows you to put it together quickly and then bake. Perfect for a multi-tasking evening!

Chicken Enchiladas

SERVES 4 - 6

- 2 C Salsa
- 1 8 oz. pkg. Cream Cheese, cubed
- 1 1/2 lb. or 2 C Boneless Skinless Chicken (cooked and cubed)
- 8 Flour Tortillas (8" or Fajita size)
- 1 C Cheddar Cheese, shredded
- 1 C Mozzarella Cheese, shredded
- 1 C Heavy/Whipping Cream

1. Preheat oven to 350°F.
2. Spray 9"×13" baking dish with Non-Stick Spray. In a saucepan over medium heat, stir together Salsa, Cream Cheese, and Chicken and cook, stirring occasionally until Cream Cheese melts.
3. Spoon 2 - 3 tablespoons of Chicken mixture down center of each Tortilla. Roll up Tortillas and place seam side down in a lightly greased 9"×13" baking dish.
4. Sprinkle with Cheese, and then drizzle Heavy/Whipping Cream evenly over top.
5. Bake for 30 minutes or until Cheese is completely melted.

Chicken Fajitas

SERVES 4

- 1 lb. Boneless, Skinless Chicken
- 2 T Vegetable Oil
- 2 Shallots or 1/2 Onion, thinly sliced
- 3 cloves Garlic, minced
- 1 Bell Pepper, thinly sliced
- 2 t Cumin
- 2 T Chili Powder
- 3 T Lime Juice
- Tabasco/Hot Sauce (to taste)
- 6 - 8 Flour Tortillas (8" or Fajita size)
- 1 C Cheddar Cheese, shredded

1. Thinly slice Chicken.
2. Heat Oil in fry pan. Once very hot, add Shallot/Onion, Garlic, and Peppers. Stir occasionally until vegetables are beginning to get tender, approximately 5 minutes.
3. Stir in Cumin and Chili Powder, and then add Chicken. Add Lime Juice and Tabasco, and stir occasionally until Chicken is cooked thoroughly.
4. Serve with Flour Tortillas and Cheddar Cheese. Garnish with Sour Cream and Salsa if desired.

142

Chicken Pot Pie

SERVES 4

- 1 lb. Boneless, Skinless Chicken
- 2 T Unsalted Butter
- 1/4 C Flour
- 1 15 oz. can or 2 C Chicken Broth
- 1/4 C Dried Minced Onions
- 1/2 t Salt
- Tabasco/Hot Sauce (to taste)
- 1/4 t Pepper
- 1 t Poultry Seasoning
- 1 15 oz. can Corn
- 1 C Frozen Peas, Green Beans, or Broccoli (thawed and drained)
- 1/2 C Mozzarella Cheese
- 1/2 C Cheddar Cheese, shredded
- 1 sheet Puff Pastry, thawed

1. Preheat oven to 400°F. Cut Chicken into 1" cubes.
2. In a stock pot over medium heat, melt Butter. Add Chicken and begin to cook. Sprinkle with Flour and stir until Chicken is completely cooked. Stir in Chicken Broth and continue to stir until mixture thickens.
3. Add Dried Minced Onions, Salt, Tabasco, Pepper, and Poultry Seasoning. Stir in Corn and vegetables and continue to cook for another 5 – 10 minutes.
4. In the bottom of an 8" square baking dish, sprinkle Cheeses. Pour in the Chicken mixture. Lay Puff Pastry sheet over the top of the baking dish.
5. Bake for 40 minutes. Let set a few minutes before serving.

Chicken Saltimbocca ^{SK}

SERVES 8

- 8 Boneless Skinless Chicken Breasts
- 1 t Salt
- 1/2 t Pepper
- 2 C Frozen Spinach, thawed and squeezed dry
- 1/2 C Mozzarella Cheese
- 1/2 C Parmesan Cheese
- 2 cloves Garlic, minced
- 1/4 C Olive Oil
- 1/3 C Chicken Broth

1. Preheat oven to 375°F. Place Chicken between two pieces of Plastic Wrap. Pound Chicken with a mallet or rolling pin until 1/4" thick. Salt and Pepper both sides of Chicken.
2. In a mixing bowl, combine Spinach, Cheeses, and Garlic.
3. Spread 1/8 of Spinach mixture on each Chicken Breast. Roll up, starting with a short end, and secure with a toothpick.
4. Place bundled Chicken in 9"x13" baking dish, drizzle with Olive Oil and Chicken Broth, and bake, uncovered, for 40 minutes or until cooked through.

AVOID CHICKEN OR STEAK JERKY!
You will notice that when we bake chicken or flank steak, we often drizzle the meat with olive oil and/or broth. Boneless skinless chicken and lean flank steak need additional fat/liquid to protect them from the dry heat of the oven. By adding olive oil or broth, it helps keep them tender and juicy!

144

Chicken Satay

SERVES 4
- 1 lb. Boneless, Skinless Chicken Breasts (also great with Flank Steak)

THAI PEANUT MARINADE
- 3/4 C Peanut Butter
- 1/3 C Soy Sauce
- 1/4 C Honey
- 1 1/2 T Lemon Juice
- 1 T Ginger
- 1 clove Garlic, minced
- 1/4 t Tabasco/Hot Sauce (or to taste)

1. Cut Chicken lengthwise into 1 - 2" wide strips.
2. Whisk together THAI PEANUT MARINADE ingredients. Pour into Resealable Storage Bag. Add Chicken and marinate. Allow to marinate for 1 to 4 hours.
3. In the meantime soak Wooden Skewers in water to keep Skewers from catching fire while grilling.
4. Skewer pieces of Chicken lengthwise onto Skewers. Grill Chicken Skewers, flipping 1 time, until Chicken is cooked through.

NOT AUTHENTIC, BUT DELICIOUS!
We would never claim that our recipes are completely authentic. It is more important to us to create great tasting recipes with the essence of the ethnicity, using the ingredients we already have "Stocked". This Chicken Satay is wonderful with our Thai Peanut Noodles. They both use versions of the same sauce which saves you a step. Add our Ginger Salad and you have a delicious Asian meal.

Chicken Strips

SERVES 6

- 1 lb. Boneless, Skinless Chicken Breasts
- 1/2 C Milk
- 2 t Lemon Juice
- 8 dashes Tabasco/Hot Sauce
- 1/2 C Butter Crackers
- 1/2 C Plain Bread Crumbs
- 1 t Grill Seasonings

HONEY MUSTARD DIPPING SAUCE
- 1/2 C Mayonnaise
- 2 T Yellow Mustard
- 2 T Honey
- 1 t Lemon Juice

1. Preheat oven to 425°F. Cut Chicken lengthwise into 1 - 2" wide strips.
2. Whisk together Milk, Lemon Juice, and Tabasco Sauce in a mixing bowl. Add Chicken and toss with Milk mixture until Chicken is coated.
3. In a Resealable Storage Bag, place Crackers and seal. Finely crush Crackers with a rolling pin.   Add to the Crackers the Bread Crumbs and Grill Seasonings.
4. Remove the Chicken from the Milk with a slotted spoon and place Chicken in bag with crumb mixture. Seal bag and shake to coat Chicken.
5. Place the Chicken on a Parchment Paper covered jelly roll pan.
6. Bake for 20 minutes. Check the center of the thickest piece of chicken to make sure it's cooked through.
7. Mix together HONEY MUSTARD DIPPING SAUCE ingredients and serve with warm Chicken Strips.

GROWN-UP CHICKEN STRIPS
Chicken Strips are often found on the "kid's menu" but these flavorful Strips are great for everyone! To give them a more adult presentation, use them to top a salad or wrap them in a flour tortilla with lettuce, tomato slices, and a drizzle of Honey Mustard Dipping Sauce!

146

Feta Chicken

SERVES 4

- 1 1/2 lb. Boneless Skinless Chicken
- 2 C Frozen Chopped Spinach, thawed and squeezed dry
- Grill Seasoning (to taste)
- 3 T Lemon Juice
- 4 oz. Feta Cheese
- 1 Roasted Red Pepper, diced (or substitute Bell Pepper)

1. Preheat oven to 350°F. Spray a 9"x13" baking dish with Non-Stick Spray.
2. Spread Spinach on bottom of baking dish.
3. Sprinkle each side of Chicken with Grill Seasoning and lay over Spinach.
4. Top with Feta Cheese and Red Pepper and drizzle with Lemon Juice.
5. Bake uncovered for 35 to 40 minutes or until Chicken is fully cooked.

AND A SIDE OF EGG NOODLES
Pasta and egg noodles can be an excellent side dish without a recipe. Cook them according to their package directions. Drain and stir in 1 - 2 T of unsalted butter or olive oil. Sprinkle with parmesan, feta, or bleu cheese and serve. Olive oil and feta cheese are delicious with this Feta Chicken recipe.

Ginger Broccoli Stir Fry

SERVES 4

- 1 lb. Boneless, Skinless Chicken
- 1 T Ginger
- 1 T Soy Sauce
- 1/2 C Chicken Broth
- 1 T Vegetable Oil
- 2 cloves Garlic, minced
- 1 16 oz. pkg. Frozen Broccoli
- 1/4 C Peanuts, chopped

1. Cut Chicken into thin strips.
2. Mix together Ginger, Soy Sauce, and Chicken Broth and set aside.
3. In a fry pan, heat Oil until very hot. Add Chicken to pan. Add Garlic and stir fry until meat is cooked through.
4. Add Broccoli and turn down heat to medium low. Stir in Soy Sauce mixture, and cook until Broccoli is heated through, about 5 - 10 minutes. Serve with cooked Rice.

Mexican Chicken

SERVES 4

- 1 lb. Boneless, Skinless Chicken
- 1/2 C Salsa
- 1/4 C Sour Cream/Plain Yogurt
- 1/2 C Tortilla Chips, crushed
- 1/2 C Cheddar Cheese, shredded
- 1/4 C Black Olives, chopped or sliced

1. Preheat oven to 375°F.
2. Spray an 8" square baking dish with Non-Stick Spray and lay in Chicken. While in baking dish, slice Chicken three times across the top to open them up and allow the flavors to penetrate.
3. Mix together Salsa and Sour Cream. Spread Chicken with Salsa mixture and sprinkle with Tortilla Chips.
4. Bake uncovered for 20 minutes. Remove from oven, sprinkle with Cheese and Olives and bake for another 10 minutes or until Chicken is cooked through.

148

Nutty Chicken

SERVES 4

- 1 lb. Boneless Skinless Chicken
- 1 t Salt
- 1/2 t Pepper
- 2 T Mayonnaise
- 2 T Dijon Mustard
- 1/2 C Almonds, Pecans, or Pine Nuts (finely chopped)

1. Preheat oven to 375°F.
2. Spray an 8" square baking dish with Non-Stick Spray and lay in Chicken and sprinkle with Salt and Pepper.
3. Mix Mayonnaise and Mustard until blended. Spread on top of Chicken. Sprinkle with Nuts.
4. Bake 20 - 25 minutes or until Chicken is cooked through.

BAKED DISHES FOR GUESTS
These Chicken bakes are ideal for guests. They taste great and since they're baked, you can actually enjoy your guests company before dinner. Use 1 Chicken Breast or 2 Chicken Thighs per guest and increase the recipe accordingly.

Sweet and Sour Stir Fry

SERVES 4

- 1 lb. Boneless, Skinless Chicken
- 2 T Soy Sauce
- 2 T Balsamic Vinegar
- 1 T Brown Sugar
- 1/4 t Red Pepper Flakes (or to taste)
- 2 T Vegetable Oil
- 1 Bell Pepper, cut into 1" chunks
- 1/2 C Shallot/Onions, diced
- 1 15 oz. can Pineapple, drained

1. Cut Chicken into thin slices.
2. Mix together Soy Sauce, Balsamic Vinegar, Brown Sugar, and Red Pepper Flakes and set aside.
3. Heat a fry pan over high heat. Add Oil and heat until very hot. Add Chicken, Bell Pepper, and Shallot/Onions and cook until Chicken is cooked through and vegetables are soft.
4. Add Pineapple and Sauce Mixture and stir to coat and to warm through.
5. Serve with cooked Rice or Flour Tortillas.

150

Southwest Chicken and Rice SK

SERVES 4

- 1 C Rice, uncooked
- 1 15 oz. can Black Beans, rinsed and drained
- 1 15 oz. can Corn, drained
- 1 15 oz. can Diced Tomatoes
- 2 C Water
- 2 T Dried Minced Onions
- 1 1/2 t Salt
- 1 T Chili Powder
- 1/2 t Garlic Powder
- 1 lb. Boneless, Skinless Chicken
- 1 C Cheddar Cheese, shredded

1. Preheat the oven to 375°F.
2. Combine Rice, Beans, Corn, Tomatoes, Water, Minced Onions, Salt, Chili Powder, and Garlic Powder and spread in the bottom of a greased 9"x13" baking dish. Top with Chicken and cover Chicken with Cheese.
3. Cover pan with Aluminum Foil or lid and bake for 40-45 minutes or until Chicken and Rice are completely cooked.

FLANK STEAK / FLAT IRON STEAK

These are cost effective and lean cuts of steak. The following cooking methods are all great with marinated meat. (See our marinade recipes.) When marinating the meat, make sure to score or cut the meat about 1/8th of an inch deep against the grain across the entire piece. A one and a half pound flank steak will generally serve 4 - 6. These steaks are best when cut in thin slices against the grain and then served. Try serving topped with our homemade Salsa recipes.

Broil:
(If you don't have a broiling pan, cover your jelly roll pan with Aluminum Foil and then top with a cooling rack.)
1. Season your Steak on both sides with Grill Seasoning.
2. Turn on your broiler and allow to broil for about 7 minutes on each side or to desired temperature.

Grill:
1. Season Steak with Grill Seasoning and place on preheated grill. The grill should be at a medium heat.
2. Grill for approximately 9 minutes on each side or to desired temperature.

Simmer:
1. In a large fry pan heated to medium high, place about a tablespoon of Olive Oil.
2. Season meat on both sides with Grill Seasoning. (If steak is marinated, just add Steak and marinade to fry pan and simmer covered for 1 1/2 hours.)
3. Lightly brown both sides of Steak in the pan.
4. Add 1 C of Beef Broth to pan, reduce heat, cover, and let simmer for approximately 1 1/2 hours until fork tender.

152

Black and Bleu Roll-Up SK

SERVES 4 - 6

- 1 1/2 lbs. Flank Steak/Flat Iron Steak
- 2 T Grill Seasoning
- 1/2 C Bleu/Gorgonzola Cheese
- 1/2 C Cream Cheese
- 1 T Dried Minced Onions
- 3 T Prepared Horseradish
- 1 T Olive OIl
- 1/2 C Beef Broth

1. Preheat oven to 375°F. Pound Steak out to help tenderize. It is best if meat is at room temperature before cooking. Season both sides lightly with Grill Seasoning.
2. Mix together Bleu Cheese, Cream Cheese, Minced Onions, and Horseradish and spread over Flank Steak. Roll up Steak, starting with short end, and secure with Toothpicks.
3. Lay in an 8" square baking dish. Drizzle Olive Oil over top and pour Beef Broth in bottom of baking dish. Cover with Aluminum Foil and bake for 60 minutes or until cooked to desired temperature. Let set for a couple of minutes before slicing.

MARINATED BLACK AND BLEU ROLL-UP
Try marinating this meat with our Italian Marinade recipe first. Instead of topping with olive oil and beef broth, simply pour the remaining marinade over the top of the rolled-up steak. Then season with grill seasoning. Bake according to directions above.

Braised Provençal Steak (or Chicken)

SERVES 4 - 6

- 2 T Flour
- 1 t Salt
- 1/4 t Pepper
- 1 1/2 - 2 lbs. Flank Steak, cubed (or whole Chicken Breasts)
- 2 T Olive Oil
- 2 cloves Garlic, minced
- 1/4 C Shallot or 1/2 C Onion, diced
- 1 C Carrots, chopped

- 1 C Celery, chopped
- 1 15 oz. can Diced Tomatoes
- 1 15 oz. can or 2 C Beef Broth (Chicken Broth for Chicken)
- 1/4 C Balsamic Vinegar
- 1 t Salt
- 1 T Herbes de Provence
- 1/4 C Flour
- 1/2 C Cold Water

1. Mix together 2 T of Flour, 1 t Salt, and Pepper in a Resealable Storage Bag. Toss in Flank Steak (or Chicken), seal bag, and shake to coat.

2. Heat Olive Oil in stock pot over medium heat. Remove Steak (or Chicken) from bag and brown on all sides for about 2-3 minutes.

3. Over top of Steak, add Garlic, Shallot/Onion, Carrots, Celery, Diced Tomatoes, Broth, Balsamic Vinegar, Salt, and Herbes de Provence. Cook on medium high for about 10 minutes, and then reduce heat to low and cover. Simmer for 1 1/2 hours.

4. Mix remaining 2 T Flour with Cold Water and stir until combined to make a thickener. (If using Chicken, remove from pot and plate.) Slowly stir in Flour mixture into the pot, cooking over low heat until "gravy" is desired thickness.

5. Serve over Egg Noodles or Mashed Potatoes. (For Chicken, scoop some of gravy and vegetable mix over plated Chicken and serve.)

Greek Roll-Up SK

SERVES 4 - 6

- 1 1/2 lbs. Flank Steak/Flat Iron Steak
- 2 T Grill Seasoning
- 1 clove Garlic, minced
- 1/4 t Salt
- 1/4 C Shallot or 1/2 C Onion, finely diced
- 1/4 C Plain Bread Crumbs
- 2 C Frozen Spinach, thawed and squeezed dry
- 1/4 C Feta Cheese
- 1 T Olive OIl
- 1/2 C Beef Broth

1. Preheat oven to 375°F. Pound Steak out to help tenderize. It is best if meat is at room temperature before cooking. Season both sides lightly with Grill Seasoning.
2. Mix together Garlic, Salt, Shallot, Bread Crumbs, Spinach, and Feta and spread over Flank Steak. Roll up Steak, starting with short end, and secure with Toothpicks.
3. Lay in an 8" square baking dish. Drizzle Olive Oil over top and pour Beef Broth in bottom of baking dish. Cover with Aluminum Foil and bake for 60 minutes or until cooked to desired temperature. Let set for a couple of minutes before slicing.

MARINATED GREEK ROLL-UP
Try marinating this meat with our Greek Marinade recipe first. Instead of topping with olive oil and beef broth, simply pour the remaining marinade over the top of the rolled-up steak. Then season with grill seasoning. Bake according to directions above.

Jerk Rubbed Steak

SERVES 4 - 6

- 1 1/2 lbs. Flank Steak/Flat Iron Steak
- 2 T Olive Oil
- 2 T Dried Minced Onions
- 2 t Poultry Seasoning
- 2 t Brown Sugar
- 2 t Salt
- 1 t Pumpkin Pie Spice
- 1 t Pepper
- 1/4 t Tabasco/Hot Sauce (or to taste)

1. Pound meat thoroughly to tenderize. With a sharp knife slice 1/4 inch deep cuts every inch across the grain of the meat.
2. Mix together remaining ingredients into a paste. Rub over both sides of Steak.
3. Grill over a medium low heat until cooked to desired temperature.

RUBS
Rubs are a combination of seasonings and herbs that are literally rubbed over raw meat before cooking. They provide a lot of taste and texture to your grilled steak. It is best to grill at a lower temperature with rubs so that the meat is cooked slower for more tenderness, and so that the sugars in the rubs are not scorched.

156

Moroccan Roll-Up SK

SERVES 4 - 6

- 1 1/2 lbs. Flank Steak/Flat Iron Steak
- 2 T Grill Seasoning
- 4 cloves Garlic, peeled
- 1/2 C Green/Calamata Olives
- 1/2 C Raisins
- 2 T Herbes de Provence

- 2 T Lemon Juice
- 2 T Olive Oil
- 1/4 t Salt
- 1/4 t Pepper (or to taste)
- 1 T Olive Oil
- 1/2 C Beef Broth

1. Preheat oven to 375°F. Pound Steak out to help tenderize. It is best if meat is at room temperature before cooking. Season both sides lightly with Grill Seasoning.
2. In a blender or food processor, blend together Garlic, Olives, Raisins, Herbes de Provence, Lemon Juice, Olive Oil, Salt, and Pepper. Spread over Flank Steak. Roll up Steak, starting with short end, and secure with Toothpicks.
3. Lay in an 8" square baking dish. Drizzle Olive Oil over top and pour Beef Broth in bottom of baking dish. Cover with Aluminum Foil and bake for 60 minutes or until cooked to desired temperature. Let set for a couple of minutes before slicing.

MARINATED MOROCCAN ROLL-UPS
Try marinating this meat with our Moroccan Marinade recipe first. Instead of topping with olive oil and beef broth, simply pour the remaining marinade over the top of the rolled-up steak. Then season with grill seasoning. Bake according to directions above.

Pepper and Fennel Rubbed Steak

SERVES 4 - 6

- 1 1/2 lbs. Flank Steak/Flat Iron Steak
- 1 T Olive Oil
- 1 t Pepper
- 1 T Salt
- 1 T Anise Seed/Fennel Seed, crushed
- 1/2 t Garlic Powder

1. Pound meat thoroughly to tenderize. With a sharp knife slice 1/4 inch deep cuts every inch across the grain of the meat.
2. Mix together remaining ingredients into a paste. Rub over both sides of Steak.
3. Grill over a medium low heat until cooked to desired temperature.

158

Pepper Steak

SERVES 4 - 6

- 1 1/2 lbs. Flank Steak/Flat Iron Steak, grilled or broiled
- 2 T Flour
- 1 T Water
- 1 C Beef Broth
- 1 t Salt
- 2 T White Wine Vinegar
- 3 T Vegetable Oil
- 4 cloves Garlic, minced
- 2 T Ginger
- 4 oz. can Mushrooms, drained
- 1 Bell Pepper, sliced into strips
- 1/2 C Shallot/Onion, thinly sliced
- 1/4 C Almonds, chopped

1. Pound meat thoroughly to tenderize and season both sides with Salt and Pepper. Broil or grill Steak to desired temperature.
2. Whisk together Flour and Water. Whisk in Beef Broth, Salt, and Vinegar and set aside.
3. In a large fry pan, heat Oil over medium-low heat. Add Garlic, Ginger, Mushrooms, Bell Pepper strips, and Shallot/Onions. Cook until just tender, about 3 minutes. Add Almonds and Broth mixture. Cook until thickened.
4. Slice Steak diagonally across the grain, into very thin slices, and place on a platter.
5. Pour Pepper mixture over top of Steak and serve with cooked Rice, Egg Noodles, or Mashed Potatoes.

Pesto Roll-Up SK

SERVES 4 - 6

- 1 1/2 lbs. Flank Steak/Flat Iron Steak
- 2 T Grill Seasoning
- 1 C Fresh Basil
- 3 T Pine Nuts
- 1/4 C Parmesan Cheese
- 2 cloves Garlic, peeled
- 1/4 C Olive Oil
- 1/4 t Salt
- 1/8 t Pepper (or to taste)
- 1 T Olive Oil
- 1/2 C Beef Broth

1. Preheat oven to 375°F. Pound Steak out to help tenderize. It is best if meat is at room temperature before cooking. Season both sides lightly with Grill Seasoning.
2. In a blender or food processor, blend together Basil, Pine Nuts, Parmesan, Garlic, Olive Oil, Salt, and Pepper. Spread over Flank Steak. Roll up Steak, starting with short end, and secure with Toothpicks.
3. Lay in an 8" square baking dish. Drizzle Olive Oil over top and pour Beef Broth into bottom of baking dish. Cover with Aluminum Foil and bake for 60 minutes or until cooked to desired temperature. Let set for a couple of minutes before slicing.

MARINATED PESTO ROLL-UPS
Try marinating this meat with our Italian Marinade recipe first. Instead of topping with olive oil and beef broth, simply pour the remaining marinade over the top of the rolled-up steak. Then season with grill seasoning. Bake according to directions above.

160

Steak Fajitas

SERVES 4

- 1 lb. Flank Steak/Flat Iron Steak
- 2 T Vegetable Oil
- 2 Shallots or 1/2 Onion, thinly sliced
- 3 cloves Garlic, minced
- 1 Bell Pepper, thinly sliced
- 2 t Cumin
- 2 T Chili Powder
- 3 T Lime Juice
- Tabasco/Hot Sauce (to taste)
- 6 - 8 Flour Tortillas (8" or Fajita size)
- 1 C Cheddar Cheese, shredded

1. Thinly slice Steak against the grain.
2. Heat Oil in fry pan. Once very hot, add Shallot/Onion, Garlic, and Peppers. Stir occasionally until vegetables are beginning to get tender, approximately 5 minutes.
3. Stir in Cumin and Chili Powder, and then add Steak. Add Lime Juice and Tabasco, and stir occasionally until Steak is cooked to desired temperature.
4. Serve with Flour Tortillas and Cheddar Cheese. Garnish with Sour Cream and Salsa if desired.

FIESTA!
These Fajitas are delicious with steak, chicken, or shrimp. (See chicken and shrimp sections for recipes.) Make it a complete meal with our Spanish Rice recipe and our Catalina Salad!

Steak and Potato Shish Kebab

- 1.5 lb. Flank Steak, cubed into 1" pieces
- 2 Potatoes, scrubbed well
- 1 Bell Pepper, cut into 1 1/2" chunks
- 2 Shallots or 1 Onion, cut into 1 1/2" chunks

JAVA MARINADE
- 3 T Worcestershire sauce
- 1/2 C Coffee, strongly brewed and cooled
- 1/4 C Vegetable Oil
- 3 T Balsamic Vinegar
- 3 T Brown Sugar
- 2 t Salt
- 1/2 t Pepper
- 1 clove Garlic, minced
- 1 T Ginger

1. Place Potatoes in stock pot and cover with water. Bring to a boil and parboil for 3 - 5 minutes or until just fork tender. Cut into 1 1/2" chunks.
2. Whisk together JAVA MARINADE ingredients. Split between two Resealable Storage Bags. Place Steak in one and Potatoes, Peppers, and Shallots/Onions in the other and marinate for at least 1 hour. (If you don't have the time, marinate for as long as you can.)
3. In the meantime soak Wooden Skewers in water to keep Skewers from catching fire while grilling.
4. Skewer pieces of Steak, Potato, Bell Peppers, and Shallot/Onion in desired pattern onto 6 - 8 Wooden Skewers. Grill skewers until Steak is cooked to desired temperature.

PARBOILING POTATOES
Parboiling is a technique where the ingredient is partially boiled in order to finish cooking at a later time. Parboiling potatoes helps to cook the potato fully without scorching the outside.

162

Steak Wellington

SERVES 4 - 6

- 1 1/2 lbs. Flank/Flat Iron Steak
- 1 T Grill Seasoning
- 1 4 oz. can Mushrooms, well drained and finely chopped
- 1/4 C Dried Minced Onions
- 1 T Worcestershire Sauce
- 1 C Bleu/Gorgonzola Cheese
- 1 sheet Puff Pastry, thawed

STEAK SAUCE
- 3 T Ketchup
- 3 T Worcestershire Sauce
- 1 T Maple Syrup
- 1 T Chili Powder
- 1 t Prepared Horseradish

1. Preheat oven to 425°F. Pound meat thoroughly to tenderize. Sprinkle both sides with Grill Seasoning and grill or broil for approximately 4 minutes per side or until medium rare. Slice meat against the grain into very thin slices.
2. Mix together Mushrooms, Dried Minced Onions, Worcestershire Sauce, and Bleu Cheese. Set aside.
3. Roll out Puff Pastry into a 10"x14" rectangle. Spread half of the Mushroom mixture over center of Puff Pastry leaving approximately 3 inches around edges of pastry without mixture.
4. Lay half of the Steak slices over Mushroom mixture. Top Steak with remaining Mushroom mixture and then remaining Steak.
5. Fold short ends of Puff Pastry up and then sides, one at a time, of Puff Pastry so that Mushroom mixture and Steak are completely contained.
6. Bake for 25 minutes or until pastry is golden brown. Let sit for a few minutes.
7. Mix together STEAK SAUCE ingredients and serve with slices of Steak Wellington.

GROUND BEEF
All of these recipes work great with ground beef, turkey, or chicken.

Beef Enchiladas SK

Serves 4 - 6

TACO MEAT
- 1 lb. Ground Beef
- 2 T Flour
- 1 T Chili Powder
- 1 t Salt
- 1 t Dried Minced Onions
- 1/2 t Garlic Powder
- 1/2 t Cumin
- 1/2 C Water

ENCHILADA SAUCE
- 3 T Chili Powder
- 3 T Flour
- 1 t Cocoa Powder
- 1/2 t Garlic Powder
- 1/2 t Salt
- 1 t Cumin
- 2 C Water
- 1 15 oz. can Tomato Sauce

- 8 Flour Tortillas (8" or Fajita size)
- 2 C Cheddar Cheese, shredded
- 1/2 C Olives, chopped (optional)
- 1/2 C Green Onions, sliced (optional)

1. Cook Ground Beef thoroughly and drain. In a mixing bowl combine remaining TACO MEAT ingredients. Over low heat mix in seasoning combination and Water. Simmer for a few minutes, until mixed well.
2. For ENCHILADA SAUCE, combine all dry ingredients and a couple of tablespoons of Water to make a paste. Scoop mixture into a saucepan and add the remaining Water. Cook over medium heat, stirring occasionally until mixture thickens, about 5 minutes. Remove from heat and stir in Tomato Sauce.
3. Preheat oven to 350°F. Spray a 9"x13" baking dish with Non-Stick Spray. Spread about 1/2 C of ENCHILADA SAUCE on bottom of baking dish.
4. Fill each Tortilla with TACO MEAT mixture and fold up like a burrito. Place filled Tortillas, seam down, into pan. Cover with remaining ENCHILADA SAUCE. Sprinkle on Cheese, Olives, and Green Onions. Bake for 30 minutes or until Cheese is completely melted.

164

Beef Nachos

- 1 lb. Ground Beef
- 2 T Flour
- 1 T Chili Powder
- 1 t Salt
- 1 t Dried Minced Onions
- 1/2 t Garlic Powder

- 1/2 t Cumin
- 1/2 C Water
- Tortilla Chips
- 1 C Black Beans, drained and rinsed
- 1 Tomato, diced
- 2 C Cheddar Cheese

1. Preheat oven to 350°F.
2. In a fry pan cook meat thoroughly, drain, and return to fry pan.
3. In a mixing bowl combine Flour, Chili Powder, Salt, Dried Minced Onions, Garlic Powder, and Cumin.
4. Stir in mix and Water with Ground Beef and simmer for a few minutes.
5. On an Aluminum Foil covered jelly roll pan, arrange desired amount of Tortilla Chips. Top with Ground Beef mixture, Black Beans, Cheese, and Tomatoes.
6. Bake for 15 - 20 minutes or until Cheese is melted and beginning to brown.
7. Serve with Salsa and Sour Cream if desired.

Greek Burger

SERVES 4

- 1 lb. Ground Beef
- 1 clove Garlic, minced
- 1 t Herbes de Provence
- 1 T Dried Minced Onions
- 1 t Salt
- 1/4 t Cinnamon
- 2 T Sour Cream/Plain Yogurt
- 2 Pita Bread
- 1/2 C Feta Cheese
- Tomato, diced (optional)
- Green/Calamata Olives, chopped
(optional)

CUCUMBER SAUCE
- 1/2 English Cucumber, finely diced
- 3/4 C Sour Cream/Plain Yogurt
- 1/8 t Garlic Powder
- 1/2 t Dill Weed
- 1/4 t Salt

1. Mix together Ground Beef with 1 clove of minced Garlic, Herbes de Provence, Dried Minced Onions, Salt, Cinnamon, and 2 T Sour Cream/Plain Yogurt. Form 4 patties and pan fry or grill to desired temperature.
2. Cut Pita in half and stuff with cooked burger patty, Feta Cheese, Tomatoes, and Olives.
3. Mix together CUCUMBER SAUCE ingredients. Spoon over burgers and serve.

166

Italian Burger

SERVES 4

- 1 lb. Ground Beef
- 1 clove Garlic, minced
- 1 T Unsalted Butter, melted
- 1 t Salt
- 1/2 t Pepper
- 1 T Italian Seasonings
- 1 t Dried Minced Onions
- 1/2 C Mozzarella
- Lettuce (optional)
- Tomato, sliced (optional)

PESTO MAYONNAISE
- 1/2 C Fresh Basil Leaves
- 2 T Pine Nuts
- 1/4 C Parmesan Cheese
- 1 clove Garlic, coarsely chopped
- 1/4 C Mayonnaise

1. Mix together Ground Beef with Garlic, melted Butter, Salt, Pepper, Italian Seasonings, and Dried Minced Onions. Form four hamburger patties and begin to pan fry or grill. When burgers are just about cooked through, top with Cheese, and allow cheese to melt.
2. In a food processor or blender, pulse PESTO MAYONNAISE ingredients together until smooth.
3. Serve Burgers on a Hamburger Bun (recipe below) topped with our PESTO MAYONNAISE, Lettuce, and Tomato slices.

Hamburger Bun

- 1 loaf Frozen Bread Dough, thawed

1. Cut thawed Bread Dough into 6 pieces. Roll chunks into balls. Place on a Parchment Paper covered jelly roll pan. Cover with greased Plastic Wrap and allow to double in size (takes 2-4 hours).
2. Remove Plastic Wrap and bake at 350°F for 20 minutes.

Meatballs

SERVES 4

- 1 lb. Ground Beef
- 1/2 C Plain Bread Crumbs
- 1 T Italian Seasonings
- 2 Eggs, lightly beaten
- 2 T Dried Minced Onions
- 1 t Salt
- 1/4 t Pepper

1. Mix all ingredients with meat. (Use your hands.)
2. Roll into 2 inch balls.
3. Cook in boiling sauce (like our Marinara Sauce recipe) for 30 minutes. You can also bake at 375°F for 20 - 25 minutes on a foil lined jelly roll pan topped with a cooling rack.

A SPICY MEAT-A-BALL

Doubling or tripling this recipe doesn't add much, if any, extra effort. We, at least, double the recipe and then freeze the Meatballs. We can then toss them into any of our "Meatball Sauces" for a quick meal or appetizer.

168

Meatloaf

SERVES 4

- 1/4 C Milk
- 3 slices Bread
- 1 lb. Ground Beef
- 1/4 C Ketchup
- 1 t Worcestershire Sauce
- 2 t Dijon Mustard
- 1 Egg, lightly beaten
- 1 T Dried Minced Onions
- 1/2 t Salt
- 1/4 t Pepper
- 1/4 C Brown Sugar
- 1 t Yellow Mustard
- 1/2 C Ketchup

1. Preheat oven to 400°F. Pour Milk into a mixing bowl. Add Bread slices and allow them to absorb the Milk.
2. Add Ground Beef, 1/4 C Ketchup, Worcestershire Sauce, Mustard, Egg, Dried Minced Onions, Salt, and Pepper and mix together well. (It is easiest to use hands.) Press mixture into a greased loaf pan.
3. Combine remaining ingredients and spread over the top of the Meatloaf.
4. Bake for 35 - 45 minutes. Remove from pan to drain off grease. Slice and serve.

COMFORT FOOD
Meatloaf is comfort food at its best. Serve this recipe with one of our Mashed Potato recipes, and our Corn Casserole for a hearty, delicious meal.

Sloppy Joes (SK)

SERVES 4

- 1 lb. Ground Beef, Turkey, or Chicken
- 1 T Dried Minced Onions
- 3/4 t Salt
- 1 T Worcestershire Sauce
- 2/3 C Ketchup
- 1/4 C Brown Sugar
- 1 T Yellow Mustard
- 1 T Barbecue Sauce

1. In a fry pan cook ground meat thoroughly, drain, and return to fry pan.
2. Mix in remaining ingredients and simmer, stirring often, for 20 minutes. Serve on Bread, Pita Bread, or our Hamburger Bun (recipe below).

Hamburger Bun

- 1 loaf Frozen Bread Dough, thawed

1. Cut thawed Bread Dough into 6 pieces.
2. Roll chunks into balls. Place on a Parchment Paper covered jelly roll pan.
3. Cover with greased Plastic Wrap and allow to double in size (takes 2-4 hours).
4. Remove Plastic Wrap and bake at 350°F for 20 minutes.

Southwest Burger

SERVES 6

- 1 lb. Ground Beef
- 1 T Chili Powder
- 1 t Salt
- 1 t Dried Minced Onions
- 1/2 t Garlic Powder
- 1/2 t Cumin
- 2 T Sour Cream/Plain Yogurt
- 1/2 C Cheddar Cheese
- 4 Flour Tortillas (8" or Fajita size)
- Lettuce (optional)
- Tomato, sliced (optional)
- Black Olives (optional)

CAJUN AIOLI
- 1 C Mayonnaise
- 12 drops Tabasco/Hot Sauce
- 1/2 t Garlic Powder
- 1 T Chili Powder
- 1/2 T Dried Minced Onions
- 1/4 t Nutmeg
- 1/2 t Pepper

1. Mix together Ground Beef with Chili Powder, Salt, Minced Onions, Garlic Powder, Cumin, and Sour Cream/Plain Yogurt. When burgers are just about cooked through, top with Cheese, and allow cheese to melt.
2. In a mixing bowl, combine CAJUN AIOLI recipe.
3. Serve Burgers on a Flour Tortilla, topped with CAJUN AIOLI, Lettuce, Tomato slices, and Olives.

Taco Meat SK

SERVES 4

- 1 lb. Ground Beef
- 2 T Flour
- 1 T Chili Powder
- 1 t Salt
- 1 t Dried Minced Onions
- 1/2 t Garlic Powder
- 1/2 t Cumin
- 1/2 C Water

1. In a fry pan cook ground meat thoroughly, drain, and return to fry pan.
2. In a mixing bowl combine all ingredients except water.
3. Stir in mix and water with Ground Beef and simmer for a few minutes.
4. Serve on Flour Tortillas or over Tortilla Chips.

TAKE YOUR TACO MEAT FURTHER
We love to add a can of drained and rinsed black beans to our Taco Meat to inexpensively double the recipe without adding any extra fat. This is also one of our go to recipes when we need dinner quickly. We make a Taco Salad by topping lettuce with this Taco Meat recipe, drained corn, rinsed and drained black beans, cheese, black olives, and our Salsa Ranch dressing. Our children get Taco Meat with flour tortillas and cheese. It is healthy and economical "fast food."

SEAFOOD

Our Seafood options make great meals. We toss crab meat and shrimp onto salads, pastas, or rice. For pasta dishes, we add shrimp to the sauce toward the end and save the step of cooking them separately. For an appetizer, we leave the tails on our shrimp; for entrees, we generally remove tails before cooking. DO NOT OVERCOOK SHRIMP! Only cook until pink or they become very tough.

Boil:
1. In a stock pot filled halfway with water, add a peeled clove of Garlic and ten Peppercorns.
2. Bring to a boil. Add Shrimp and cook for 2 minutes or until all Shrimp are just pink. Remove peppercorns and garlic, drain Shrimp, and serve.

Grill:
1. Soak Wooden Skewers in water for 20 - 30 minutes in a jelly roll pan to avoid burning Skewers.
2. Marinate 1 lb. of Shrimp in a Resealable Storage Bag for 1 - 2 hours in refrigerator, if desired. Skewer 4 - 6 (depending on size) Shrimp, tail end first and then the head. If you haven't marinated Shrimp, baste with a little Olive Oil and sprinkle with Grill Seasoning.
3. Place Shrimp Skewers on a hot grill for 1 or 2 minutes and then turn to other side for about 30 seconds. Shrimp will turn pink when done.

Sauteed:
1. Melt 1 - 2 T of Unsalted Butter in a fry pan. Toss in Shrimp and sauté until pink. Also, try marinating Shrimp before sauteing.

Crab Cakes SK

SERVES 4

- 2 6 oz. pkg. Crab Meat, imitation (chopped) or canned lump (drained)
- 2/3 C Bread Crumbs
- 3 Green Onions, minced
- 3 T Milk
- 3 T Mayonnaise
- 1/2 t Salt
- 1/4 t Pepper
- 2 T Unsalted Butter
- 2 - 3 T Flour

TARTAR SAUCE
- 1 C Mayonnaise
- 1 T Sweet or Dill Relish
- 1 T Dried Minced Onion
- 2 T Lemon Juice

1. Combine Crab Meat, Bread Crumbs, Green Onions, Milk, Mayonnaise, Salt, and Pepper in a mixing bowl.
2. Form small round patties with your hands, cover, and refrigerate for about 1 hour.
3. Heat fry pan over medium heat and begin to melt Butter. Pour Flour onto a plate and dip each side of Crab Cakes in Flour.
4. Place Crab Cakes in fry pan and cook until golden brown (approximately 4 - 5 minutes on each side).
5. Mix TARTAR SAUCE ingredients together and serve with warm Crab Cakes.

174

Crab Enchiladas

SERVES 4 - 6

- 2 C Salsa
- 1 8 oz. pkg. Cream Cheese, cubed
- 1 t Dill Weed (optional)
- 2 6 oz. pkg. Crab Meat, imitation (chopped) or canned lump (drained)
- 8 Flour Tortillas (8" or Fajita size)
- 1 C Cheddar Cheese, shredded
- 1 C Mozzarella Cheese, Shredded
- 1 C Heavy/Whipping Cream

1. Preheat oven to 350°F.
2. Spray 9"×13" baking dish with Non-Stick Spray. In a saucepan over medium heat, stir together Salsa, Cream Cheese, Dill, and Crab Meat and cook, stirring, until Cream Cheese melts.
3. Spoon 2-3 tablespoons of Crab mixture down center of each Tortilla. Roll up Tortillas and place seam side down in a lightly greased 9"×13" baking dish.
4. Sprinkle with Cheese and then drizzle Heavy/Whipping Cream evenly over top.
5. Bake for 30 minutes or until Cheese is completely melted.

Crab Noodle Casserole

SERVES 4

- 3 C Egg Noodles
- 2 T Unsalted Butter, melted
- 2 T Flour
- 1 C Milk
- 2 T Dried Minced Onions
- 1 4 oz. can Mushrooms
- 1 C Cheddar Cheese
- 1 6 oz. pkg. Crab Meat, imitation (chopped) or canned lump (drained)
- 1/2 C Butter Crackers, smashed

1. Preheat oven to 375°F. Spray an 8" square baking dish with Non-Stick Spray.
2. In a saucepan, cook Noodles according to package directions.
3. In a mixing bowl, whisk together Butter and Flour. Whisk in 1 - 2 tablespoons of the Milk until smooth. Add remaining Milk and whisk until smooth. Mix in Dried Minced Onions and Mushrooms.
4. Drain noodles and add to Milk mixture. Stir in Cheese and Crab and pour into baking dish.
5. Sprinkle with Butter Cracker crumbs and bake for 25 - 30 minutes or until golden brown and bubbling.

176

Lemon Pepper Shrimp

SERVES 4

- 1 Lemon
- 1 sticks Unsalted Butter, melted
- 2 t Pepper
- 1/2 t Herbes de Provence
- 1/2 t Tabasco/Hot Sauce
- 1/2 t Salt
- 1 clove Garlic, minced
- 12 oz. - 1 lb. Shrimp, raw, peeled, de-veined, de-tailed, and thawed

1. Preheat oven to 400°F.
2. Cut Lemon in half. Slice one half and juice the other half into a mixing bowl. Combine all other ingredients, except Lemon Slices and Shrimp, with Lemon juice.
3. Pour 1/4 C of sauce on bottom of an 8" square baking dish. Arrange Shrimp over top of sauce and top Shrimp with Lemon slices. Pour remaining sauce over top.
4. Bake for about 20 minutes or until all Shrimp have turned pink.
5. Great served over Rice and with fresh, warm Bread.

Mock Shrimp Ceviche (se-vē-chā) SK

SERVES 4

- 12 oz. - 1 lb. Shrimp, raw, peeled, de-veined, de-tailed, and thawed
- 1/2 C Salsa
- 1/2 T Chili Powder
- 1/2 t Salt
- 1/2 C Lime Juice
- 1 clove Garlic, minced
- 1 Green Onion, chopped
- 1 15 oz. can Black Beans, drained and rinsed
- 1/2 English Cucumber, diced

1. Bring a stock pot filled halfway with water to a boil. Cook Shrimp for 2 minutes or until pink. Remove from heat, drain, and set aside.
2. Whisk together Salsa, Chili Powder, Salt, and Lime Juice.
3. Stir in Shrimp and remaining ingredients. Chill for about 1 hour.

MOCK SHRIMP MARTINI
Wow your guests by serving this wonderful Ceviche in Martini Glasses garnished with tortilla chips or cucumber slices. It is a refreshing salad course or appetizer. Although Ceviches are technically seafood cooked in the acid of lemon or lime juice, this "Stocked" version is sure to please!

178

Moo Shoo Shrimp Stir Fry

SERVES 4

- 4 T Soy Sauce
- 1 T Peanut Butter
- 1 T Honey
- 2 t White Wine Vinegar
- 1/8 t Garlic Powder
- 10 drops Tabasco/Hot Sauce
- 1/8 t Pepper
- 2 T Ginger
- 3 Eggs, beaten
- Salt and Pepper, to taste
- 2 T Vegetable Oil
- 12 oz. - 1 lb. Shrimp, raw, peeled, de-veined, de-tailed, and thawed
- 1 clove Garlic, minced
- 1 4 oz. can Mushrooms
- 3 cups Cabbage and Carrot mix
- 3 Green Onions, sliced on angle

1. Mix together Soy Sauce, Peanut Butter, Honey, White Wine Vinegar, Garlic Powder, Tabasco Sauce, Pepper, and Ginger and set aside.
2. Beat together Eggs, Salt, and Pepper and set aside.
3. Heat a fry pan over high heat. Add Oil and heat until very hot. Add Shrimp and cook until pink.
4. Add Egg mixture to Shrimp and scramble about 2 minutes. Add Garlic, Mushrooms, Cabbage and Carrot Mix, and Green Onions and cook until Green Onions are tender.
5. Toss with Soy Sauce mixture to coat. Serve with cooked Rice or Flour Tortillas.

Pancake Battered Fried Shrimp SK

SERVES 4

- 1 1/2 C Pancake Mix
- 1 t Chili Powder
- 1/2 t Pumpkin Pie Spice
- 12 oz. - 1 lb. Shrimp, raw, peeled, de-veined, and thawed
- Vegetable Oil, for frying

TARTAR SAUCE
- 1 C Mayonnaise
- 1 T Sweet or Dill Relish
- 1 T Dried Minced Onion
- 2 T Lemon Juice

1. Separate out 1 C of Pancake Mix and prepare according to package instructions, omitting oil even if recipe calls for it. Add Chili Powder and Pumpkin Pie Spice and set aside.
2. Place remaining dry Pancake Mix in a mixing bowl and toss thawed Shrimp around until coated.
3. Heat 1/2 inch of Oil in a fry pan until very hot. Dip Shrimp in batter mix and transfer to hot Oil. Cook 1 - 2 minutes on each side until golden. Tails will turn pink.
4. Absorb grease by laying on paper towels.
5. Mix TARTAR SAUCE ingredients together and serve with warm or room temperature Shrimp.

180

Seafood Nachos

SERVES 4

- 1 6 oz. pkg. Crab Meat, imitation (chopped) or canned lump (drained)
- 1/4 C Sour Cream/Plain Yogurt
- 1/4 C Mayonnaise
- 2 T Dried Minced Onion
- 1/4 t Dill Weed
- Tortilla Chips
- 2 C Cheddar Cheese
- 1 Tomato, diced

1. In a mixing bowl combine Crab, Sour Cream/Plain Yogurt, Mayonnaise, Dried Minced Onions, and Dill Weed.
2. On an Aluminum Foil covered jelly roll pan, arrange desired amount of Tortilla Chips. Top with Fajita mixture, Cheese, and Tomatoes.
3. Bake for 15 - 20 minutes or until Cheese is melted and beginning to brown.
4. Serve with Salsa and more Sour Cream if desired.

Shrimp Cocktail

SERVES 4

- 12 oz. - 1 lb. Shrimp (raw, peeled, and de-veined), thawed
- 3 cloves Garlic, peeled
- 10 Peppercorns, whole (optional)

COCKTAIL SAUCE
- 1/2 C Ketchup
- 2 T Prepared Horseradish
- 1 T Lemon Juice

1. In a stock pot filled halfway with water, add peeled Garlic and Peppercorns. Bring to a boil. Add Shrimp and cook for 2 minutes or until all Shrimp are just pink.
2. Mix together COCKTAIL SAUCE ingredients and chill. Serve Shrimp over ice with COCKTAIL SAUCE.

Shrimp Fajitas

SERVES 4

- 12 oz. - 1 lb. Shrimp, raw, peeled, de-veined, de-tailed, and thawed
- 2 T Vegetable Oil
- 2 Shallots or 1/2 Onion, thinly sliced
- 3 cloves Garlic, minced
- 1 Bell Pepper, thinly sliced
- 2 t Cumin
- 2 T Chili Powder
- 3 T Lime Juice
- Tabasco/Hot Sauce (to taste)
- 6 - 8 Flour Tortillas (8" or Fajita size)
- 1 C Cheddar Cheese, shredded

1. Heat Oil in fry pan. Once very hot, add Shallot/Onion, Garlic, and Peppers. Stir occasionally until vegetables are beginning to get tender, approximately 5 minutes.
2. Stir in Shrimp, Cumin, and Chili Powder. Add Lime Juice and Tabasco and stir occasionally until Shrimp is cooked thoroughly and pink.
3. Serve on Flour Tortillas with Cheddar Cheese. Garnish with Sour Cream and Salsa if desired.

182

Shrimp Pineapple Shish Kebab

SERVES 4

- 12 oz. - 1 lb. Shrimp, raw, peeled, de-veined, de-tailed, and thawed
- 1 15 oz. can Pineapple, drained
- 1 Bell Pepper, cut into 1" pieces

HONEY LIME MARINADE
- 1/4 C Honey
- 2 T Vegetable Oil
- 1/4 C Lime Juice
- 1/4 t Salt
- 1/4 t Tabasco/Hot Sauce (or to taste)

1. Whisk together Honey Lime Marinade ingredients. Pour marinade into 2 Resealable Storage Bags. Add Shrimp to one and the Pineapple and Bell Pepper to the other.
2. Allow to marinade between 1 and 4 hours.
3. In the meantime soak Wooden Skewers in water to keep Skewers from catching fire while grilling.
4. Skewer pieces of Shrimp, Pineapple, and Bell Pepper onto 6 - 8 Wooden Skewers. Grill skewers, flipping one time, until Shrimp is cooked and pink.

Shrimp Scampi

SERVES 4

- 12 oz. - 1 lb. Shrimp, raw, peeled, de-veined, and thawed
- 1/4 C Unsalted Butter
- 2 cloves Garlic, minced
- 1/2 t Salt
- 1/4 t Pepper
- 1 T Lemon Juice

1. Melt Butter over medium heat in a fry pan. Add Garlic and cook until slightly softened, not brown.
2. Add Shrimp. Cook until pink. Sprinkle with Salt and Pepper.
3. Remove from heat and toss with Lemon Juice.

Beans, Potatoes, Rice, and Veggies

oven chips and oven fries

black bean burger

kidney bean tortilla lasagna

maple glazed carrots

tomatoes provencal

"stocked" paella

BEANS
We love beans because they are inexpensive, easy to use, and nutritious.

Black Bean Burger SK

SERVES 4

- 1 15 oz. can Black Beans, rinsed and drained
- 1/4 C Shallot or Onion, diced
- 1/4 C Bread Crumbs
- 2 T Salsa
- 1/4 C Corn, drained
- 1/2 C Cheddar Cheese, grated
- 1 t Cumin
- 8 drops Tabasco/Hot Sauce
- 1 t Salt
- 1/4 t Pepper (or to taste)
- 1 T Olive Oil

1. Using a potato masher, mash Beans in a mixing bowl.
2. Mix in Shallot/Onion, Bread Crumbs, Salsa, Corn, Cheese, Cumin, Tabasco Sauce, Salt, and Pepper.
3. Using moistened hand, shape Bean mixture into 3 inch patties. Refrigerate for 15 minutes to allow to set.
4. In a fry pan, heat Olive Oil on medium heat. Fry patties in Oil until golden brown, approximately 3 minutes on each side.

186

Kidney Bean Tortilla Lasagna SK

SERVES 8

- 2 15 oz. can Tomato Sauce
- 2 T Chili Powder
- 1 t Salt
- 2 T Dried Minced Onions
- 1 t Garlic Powder
- 1 t Cumin
- 2 15 oz. cans Kidney Beans, drained
- 1 4 oz. can Black Olives
- 1 4 oz. can Mushrooms
- 1 15 oz. can Corn, drained
- 6 Flour Tortillas (8" or Fajita size)
- 2 C Cheddar Cheese, grated

1. Preheat oven to 350°F. Spray a 9"x13" baking dish with Non-Stick Spray.
2. In a mixing bowl, stir together Tomato Sauce, Chili Powder, Salt, Dried Minced Onions, Garlic Powder, and Cumin. Add Beans, Olives, Mushrooms, and Corn. Pour 1 C of mixture on the bottom dish.
3. Lay two Tortillas over mixture. Spread 1/3 of Bean Mixture over Tortillas and 1/3 of Cheese. Repeat this step twice.
4. Cover with Aluminum Foil and bake for 25 minutes. Remove cover and bake for 15 more minutes or until Cheese becomes Golden Brown.

Maple Ginger Baked Beans SK

SERVES 8

- 1 T Olive Oil
- 1/2 C Shallots or 1 C Onion, diced
- 2 T Dijon Mustard
- 1/4 C Maple Syrup
- 1/4 C Ketchup
- 1/4 C Brown Sugar

- 1 T Ginger
- 3 15 oz. cans Kidney Beans
- 1/2 t Tabasco/Hot Sauce
- 1/2 t Salt
- 1/4 t Pepper

1. Preheat oven to 350°F. In a saucepan over medium heat, cook the Shallots/Onions in the Oil until softened.
2. Stir in Mustard, Syrup, Ketchup, Sugar, and Ginger to the Shallots/Onions and let cook for 5 - 10 minutes.
3. Add Beans with liquid, Tabasco, Salt, and Pepper. Pour into a 9"x13" baking dish and bake uncovered for 1 hour. Let sit for 5 - 10 minutes before serving.

Teriyaki Pork and Beans

SERVES 8

- 1 T Olive Oil
- 1/2 C Shallots or 1 C Onion, diced
- 2 T Yellow Mustard
- 1 15 oz. can Pineapple, drained
- 1 C Brown Sugar

- 1/4 C Soy Sauce
- 1 T White Wine Vinegar
- 3 cans Northern/Cannelini Beans
- 1 C Ham or Bacon (cooked), diced

1. Preheat oven to 350°F. In a large saucepan over medium heat, cook the Shallots/Onions in the Oil until softened.
2. Add Mustard, Pineapple, Sugar, Soy Sauce, and Vinegar to the Shallots/Onions and let cook for 5 - 10 minutes.
3. Stir in meat and undrained Beans. Pour into a 9"x13" baking dish. Bake uncovered for 1 hour. Let sit for 5 - 10 minutes before serving.

Tuscan Baked Cannelini Beans

Serves 8

- 1 T Olive Oil
- 1/2 C Shallots or 1 C Onion, diced
- 1 12 oz. jar Marinated Artichoke Hearts, undrained
- 2 cloves Garlic, minced
- 1 15 oz. can Diced Tomatoes
- 2 T Sugar
- 1/4 C Fresh Basil, chopped
- 1 T Dijon Mustard
- 3 cans Northern/Cannelini Beans
- 1/2 C Parmesan Cheese

1. Preheat oven to 350°F. In a saucepan over medium heat, cook the Shallots/Onions in the Oil until softened.
2. Add Artichokes, Garlic, Tomatoes with juice, Sugar, and Basil to the Shallots/Onions and let cook for 5 - 10 minutes.
3. Stir in Mustard, undrained Beans and Cheese. Pour into a 9"x13" baking dish. Bake uncovered for 1 hour. Let sit for 5 - 10 minutes before serving.

POTATOES

Potatoes are versatile ingredients with delicious results. They also stay fresh in your pantry for a long time. Choose from Russet, Sweet, or Yukon Gold for most recipes.

Baked Potatoes

SERVES 6

• 6 - 8 Potatoes

1. Preheat oven to 400°F. Scrub Potatoes under cold, running water. Prick Potatoes with a fork many times to prevent them from bursting and to shorten baking time.
2. Place on oven rack. Bake for 30 minutes. Flip Potatoes and continue to bake for 30 more minutes or until soft when squeezed.
3. Cut a cross in the top of each baked Potato, and squeeze gently to open up. Fill with your favorite toppings like Butter, Sour Cream/Plain Yogurt, Cheddar Cheese, Broccoli, and cooked Bacon.

TO WRAP OR NOT TO WRAP?

By baking potatoes without wrapping them in aluminum foil, you produce a delicious, crispy skinned potato. The skin is much softer with an aluminum foil wrapped potato because you are actually steaming them. We love the crispy skin, but it is NECESSARY to pierce them deeply with a fork quite a few times, otherwise, CABOOM! Big mess in your oven. If you would prefer, wrap them up and bake according to directions above.

190

Baked Twice Potatoes  SK

SERVES 6

- 6 - 8 Potatoes
- 1/4 C Unsalted Butter, melted
- 1/2 C Sour Cream/Plain Yogurt
- 2 T Cream Cheese

- 1 t Salt
- 1/2 t Pepper
- 1/2 C Cheddar Cheese, shredded

1. Preheat oven to 400°F. Scrub Potatoes under cold, running water. Prick Potatoes with a fork many times to prevent them from bursting and to shorten baking time.
2. Place on oven rack. Bake for 30 minutes. Flip Potatoes and continue to bake for 30 more minutes.
3. When Potatoes are done, cut lengthwise in half with a sharp knife, and spoon out soft Potato, leaving a thin layer of Potato against the skin to create a sturdier shell.
4. Place Potato skins on a Parchment Paper covered jelly roll pan, open side up. Place scooped out Potato into a mixing bowl and, using an electric hand mixer, blend with remaining ingredients.
5. Fill each skin with Potato mixture. Bake Potatoes at 400°F for 15 - 20 minutes.

MAKE AHEAD HOLIDAY MEAL
We like to prepare as much as possible ahead of time when serving a large holiday meal. These Baked Twice Potatoes are perfect for that. After filling the shells with potato mixture, freeze them. When you are ready to serve, bake potatoes at 350°F for 45 minutes. If you choose to refrigerate, bake according to directions above.

Cheddar Mashed Potatoes

SERVES 4 - 6

- 2 lbs. Potatoes (4 - 6 Russet, 6 - 8 Golden)
- 2 t Salt (or to taste)
- 2 T Butter
- 1/2 C Milk
- 1/4 t Pepper
- 1 C Cheddar Cheese, grated

1. Peel Potatoes and chop into 2 inch chunks.
2. Place in a stock pot. Just cover Potatoes with cold water and add a 1/2 t Salt.
3. Bring to a boil, reduce heat to a simmer, cover, and let cook for 15 - 20 minutes until fork tender.
4. Drain Potatoes and return to stock pot.
5. Mash Potatoes with potato masher, mix in remaining Salt and other ingredients. (Mix in more Milk, little by little, until desired consistency.)

192

Garlic Mashed Potatoes

SERVES 4 - 6

- 2 lbs. Potatoes (4 - 6 Russet, 6 - 8 Golden)
- 2 t Salt (or to taste)
- 4 oz. Cream Cheese
- 2/3 C Milk
- 1 Garlic Clove, minced
- Pepper (to taste)

1. Peel Potatoes and chop into 2 inch chunks.
2. Place in a stock pot. Just cover Potatoes with cold water and add a 1/2 t Salt.
3. Bring to a boil, reduce heat to a simmer, cover, and let cook for 15 - 20 minutes until fork tender.
4. Drain Potatoes and return to stock pot.
5. Mash Potatoes with potato masher, mix in remaining Salt and other ingredients. (Mix in more Milk, little by little, until desired consistency.)

Oven Chips

SERVES 4

- 2 lbs. Potatoes (4 - 6 Russet, 6 - 8 Golden, 2 - 3 Sweet Potatoes), peeled or unpeeled
- 1T Olive Oil
- 2 T Grill Seasonings

1. Preheat oven to 425°F. Slice Potatoes into 1/8 inch chips. Place Potatoes in stock pot and cover with water. Bring to a boil and parboil for approximately 3 minutes or until just fork tender.
2. Remove Potatoes from pot, toss with Oil, lay in a single layer on a Parchment Paper lined jelly roll pan. Sprinkle with Grill Seasoning.
3. Bake for 15 minutes, then broil for 5 minutes or until crispy.

Oven Fries

SERVES 4

- 2 lbs. Potatoes (4 - 6 Russet, 6 - 8 Golden, 2 - 3 Sweet Potatoes), peeled or unpeeled
- 1 T Olive Oil
- 2 T Grill Seasonings

1. Preheat oven to 425°F. Slice Potatoes in half lengthwise and then slice each half into 4 slices lengthwise. Place Potatoes in stock pot and cover with water. Bring to a boil and parboil for approximately 3 minutes or until just fork tender.
2. Remove Potatoes from pot, toss with Oil, lay in a single layer on a Parchment Paper lined jelly roll pan. Sprinkle with Grill Seasoning.
3. Bake for 15 minutes, then broil for 5 minutes or until crispy.

PARBOILING POTATOES

Parboiling is a technique where the ingredient is partially boiled in order to finish cooking at a later time. Parboiling Potatoes helps to cook the Potato fully without scorching the outside.

194

Potatoes Au Gratin

SERVES 4

- 4 C Potatoes, peeled and thinly sliced
- 1 C Milk
- 1/2 C Sour Cream/Plain Yogurt
- 1/2 t Garlic Powder
- 2 T Fresh Basil, chopped (optional)
- 1/4 t Salt
- 1/8 t Pepper
- 6 dashes Tabasco/Hot Sauce
- 1 C Mozzarella Cheese
- 1 C Ham, diced (optional)
- 1/3 C Parmesan Cheese

1. In a stock pot, cover Potatoes with cold water. Bring to a boil and parboil for 3 minutes, just until Potatoes start to become tender, and then drain and return Potatoes to stock pot. Preheat oven to 375°F.
2. In a mixing bowl, whisk together Milk, Sour Cream/Plain Yogurt, Garlic Powder, Basil, Salt, Pepper, and Tabasco Sauce.
3. Pour Milk mixture over Potatoes and gently toss.
4. Spoon half of Potato mixture into an 8" square baking dish coated with Non-Stick Spray. Top with half of Mozzarella (and Ham if desired). Repeat.
5. Sprinkle top with Parmesan Cheese. Cover and bake 30 minutes. Uncover and bake 15 additional minutes. Let stand 10 minutes before serving.

MEAT AND POTATOES AT ITS BEST!
Serve this recipe as a delicious side dish, or add the ham for a complete family friendly meal. Also, try substituting 1/2 C of mozzarella cheese for cheddar cheese to give the dish an added zip.

Sour Cream and Onion Mashed Potatoes

SERVES 4 - 6

- 2 lbs. Potatoes (4 - 6 Russet, 6 - 8 Golden)
- 2 t Salt (or to taste)
- 1/3 C Milk
- 1/4 C Sour Cream/Plain Yogurt
- 2 T Green Onions, thinly sliced

1. Peel Potatoes and chop into 2 inch chunks.
2. Place in a stock pot. Just cover Potatoes with cold water and add a 1/2 t Salt.
3. Bring to a boil, reduce heat to a simmer, cover, and let cook for 15 - 20 minutes until fork tender.
4. Drain Potatoes and return to stock pot.
5. Mash Potatoes with potato masher, mix in remaining Salt and other ingredients. (Mix in more Milk, little by little, until desired consistency.)

196

Sweet Mashed Potatoes

SERVES 4 - 6

- 2 lbs. Potatoes (2 - 3 large Sweet Potatoes)
- 1/2 t Salt
- 2 T Butter
- 1/2 t Pumpkin Pie Spice
- 2 T Brown Sugar
- 1/2 C Milk

1. Peel Potatoes and chop into 2 inch chunks.
2. Place in a stock pot. Just cover Potatoes with cold water and add Salt.
3. Bring to a boil, reduce heat to a simmer, cover, and let cook for 15 - 20 minutes until fork tender.
4. Drain Potatoes and return to stock pot.
5. Mash Potatoes with potato masher, mix in remaining ingredients. (Mix in more Milk, little by little, until desired consistency.)

RICE

We love these rice recipes, not only because they are delicious, but because they are just about as easy as the packets we used to buy. We now cook healthier meals without sacrificing convenience.

Black Beans and Rice

SERVES 4 - 6

- 1 T Vegetable Oil
- 1 Shallot or 1/2 Onion, finely diced
- 1 clove Garlic, minced
- 1/2 Bell Pepper, finely diced
- 1 C Rice
- 1 15 oz. can or 2 C Chicken Broth
- 1 15 oz. can Pineapple, with juice
- 1 15 oz. can Black Beans, rinsed and drained
- 1/2 t Salt
- 1/4 t Red Pepper Flakes (or to taste)

1. In a fry pan over medium heat, heat Oil and cook Shallot/Onion, Garlic, and Bell Pepper until tender. Do not burn Garlic!
2. Add Rice, Chicken Broth, Pineapple Juice, Black Beans, Salt, and Dried Red Pepper Flakes, and bring to a boil. Reduce heat to a simmer, cover, and cook for 30 minutes or until liquid is absorbed.
3. When Rice is cooked, add Pineapple and heat thoroughly.

Ginger Rice SK

SERVES 4

- 1 T Ginger (in a tube)
- 1 C Rice
- 1 15 oz. can or 2 C Chicken Broth
- 1 t Salt
- 1/4 C Green Onions, finely sliced (optional)
- 1/4 C Almonds, chopped (optional)

1. In a saucepan over medium heat, stir together Ginger, Rice, Chicken Broth, and Salt and bring to a boil. Reduce heat, cover, and simmer for 30 minutes or until liquid is absorbed.
2. When Rice is tender and all liquid is incorporated, flake with fork, and fold in Green Onions and Almonds.

Lemon Dill Rice

SERVES 4

- 1 C Rice
- 1 t Dill Weed
- 2 T Lemon Juice
- 1 t Lemon, zest
- 1 15 oz. can or 2 C Chicken Broth
- 1 t Salt

1. In a saucepan, stir together Rice, Dill Weed, Lemon Juice and Zest, Chicken Broth, and Salt. Bring to a boil.
2. Cover, reduce heat, and simmer for 30 minutes or until liquid is absorbed.

Moroccan Rice SK

SERVES 4

- 1 T Unsalted Butter
- 1 Shallot or 1/2 Onion diced
- 1 C Rice
- 1/4 C Pine Nuts
- 1 15 oz. can or 2 C Chicken Broth
- 1/2 C Water

- 1 t Pumpkin Pie Spice
- 1/2 t Salt
- 1/8 t Pepper
- 1/4 C Raisins
- 1/2 C Bacon, cooked & chopped (optional)

1. In a fry pan over medium heat, melt Butter and cook Shallot/Onion, Rice, and Pine Nuts until Shallots/Onions soften.
2. Add Broth, Water, Pumpkin Pie Spice, Salt, and Pepper and bring to a boil. Reduce heat, cover, and simmer for 30 minutes or until liquid is absorbed.
3. When Rice is tender and all liquid is incorporated, flake with a fork, fold in Bacon and Raisins, and serve.

Spanish Rice SK

SERVES 4

- 1 T Olive Oil
- 1 Shallot or 1/2 Onion, finely diced
- 1/2 Green Pepper, diced (optional)
- 1 C Rice
- 1 C Water

- 1 15 oz. can Diced Tomatoes, with juice
- 1 t Salt
- 1 T Chili Powder
- 1/2 t Garlic Powder

1. In a fry pan over medium heat, heat Olive Oil and cook Shallot/Onion and Bell Pepper until tender.
2. Add remaining ingredients and bring to a boil. Reduce heat to a simmer, cover, and cook for 30 minutes or until liquid is absorbed.

200

"Stocked" Paella SK

SERVES 6 - 8

- 1/2 lb. Ground Breakfast Sausage
- 2 T White Wine Vinegar
- 6 drops Tabasco/Hot Sauce
- 1/2 lb. Boneless, Skinless Chicken, cubed
- 1/2 Bell Pepper, chopped
- 2 Shallots or 1 Onion, chopped
- 1 clove Garlic, minced
- 1 15 oz. can Diced Tomatoes, with liquid
- 1 10 oz. can Mandarin Oranges, with liquid

- 2 T Chili Powder
- 1 t Poultry Seasoning
- 1/2 t Pumpkin Pie Spice
- 1/2 t Cumin
- 1 t Salt
- 1 C Rice
- 1 15 oz. can or 2 C Chicken Broth
- 1/2 C Frozen Peas
- 6 oz. Shrimp, raw, peeled, de-veined with tails still on

1. Preheat oven to 400°F.
2. Heat a fry pan on stove top over medium heat. Brown Sausage in pan with Vinegar and Tabasco Sauce. Add Chicken and cook thoroughly. Add Bell Pepper, Shallot/Onion, and Garlic and cook until vegetables soften.
3. In a large mixing bowl add Diced Tomatoes and Mandarin Oranges. Stir in Chili Powder, Poultry Seasoning, Pumpkin Pie Spice, Cumin, Salt, Rice, and Broth. Add Sausage and Chicken Mixture and mix well.
4. Pour into a greased, deep dish pizza pan or 9"x13" baking dish and place in preheated oven, uncovered, for 30 minutes.
5. Remove pan from oven, stir in peas, and tuck Shrimp throughout dish. Place pan back in oven and bake for 10 - 15 minutes more or until Rice is tender and Shrimp are pink.

VEGGIES

These recipes are veggies at their best. Most of them are made from frozen vegetables, so they are quick and easy.

Almond Green Beans

SERVES 4

- 3 C Frozen Green Beans
- 1 T Unsalted Butter
- 1 T Olive Oil
- 1 T Lemon Juice
- 1 T Dried Minced Onions
- 1/2 C Almonds
- 1/4 t Salt
- Pepper (to taste)

1. Cook Frozen Green Beans in a saucepan according to the package directions.
2. Drain excess water and mix with remaining ingredients over low heat until combined and warmed through.

Cheesy Broccoli

SERVES 4

- 2 T Unsalted Butter
- 2 T Flour
- 1/2 C Milk
- 1/2 t Salt
- 1/4 t Pepper
- 3 C Frozen Broccoli
- 1/2 C Cheddar Cheese, grated

1. In a saucepan over medium heat, melt Butter. Whisk in Flour and cook for 1 - 2 minutes. Whisk in Milk, Salt, and Pepper, and cook until thickened.
2. Add Frozen Broccoli and allow to cook through. Once cooked, stir in Cheese and cook until melted.

202

Corn Casserole

SERVES 8

- 4 15 oz. cans Corn
- 2 t Sugar
- 2 t Salt
- 3 Eggs, beaten
- 3 Green Onions, finely sliced

- 3 C Milk
- 2 T Butter, melted
- 12 Butter Crackers, crushed
- 1 T Herbs de Provence

1. Preheat oven to 350°F. In a blender, blend 2 undrained cans of Corn with Sugar, Salt, and Butter until smooth.
2. Pour puree into mixing bowl. Drain remaining Corn. Mix in drained Corn and remaining ingredients. Pour mixture into greased 9"x13" baking dish.
3. Bake uncovered for 1 hour or until center sets.

Creamy Spinach

SERVES 4

- 3 C Frozen Spinach
- 1 T Dried Minced Onions
- 1/2 t Garlic Powder
- 4 oz. Cream Cheese

- 1/4 C Parmesan Cheese
- 1/4 t Salt
- 1/8 t Nutmeg (optional)

1. Cook Spinach in saucepan according to the package directions.
2. Squeeze out excess water and mix with remaining ingredients over low heat until combined and warmed through.

Easy Asian Broccoli

SERVES 4

- 3 C Frozen Broccoli
- 2 T Dijon Mustard
- 2 T Soy Sauce
- 1/4 C Almonds, toasted (optional)

1. Cook Broccoli in saucepan according to the package directions.
2. Mix together Dijon Mustard and Soy Sauce. Drain excess water from Broccoli and toss with Soy Sauce mixture. Sprinkle with Almonds and serve.

Feta Peas SK

SERVES 4

- 2 C Frozen Peas
- 1/4 C Feta Cheese
- 1 T Fresh Basil, chopped
- 1/4 t Salt
- 1/8 t Pepper

1. Cook Peas in saucepan according to the package directions.
2. Drain excess water and mix with remaining ingredients over low heat until combined and warmed through.

204

Glazed Carrots

SERVES 4

- 1 T Unsalted Butter
- 4 C or 1 lb. Carrots, chopped into 1" chunks ("Baby" Carrots work as is)
- 1 C Beef Broth
- 1/4 C Maple Syrup
- 1/4 t Salt
- 1/8 t Pepper
- 1/2 C Pecans, chopped and toasted

1. In a fry pan over medium heat, melt Butter. Add Carrots and stir to coat. Add Beef Broth, Maple Syrup, Salt, and Pepper. Increase to high heat and bring to a boil. Cover and cook for approximately 8 - 10 minutes or until tender.
2. Uncover and cook until liquid reduces to a glaze over Carrots, approximately 15 - 20 minutes. Stir in Pecans and serve immediately.

Horseradish Peas

SERVES 4

- 2 C Frozen Peas
- 1/4 t Salt
- 1 T Unsalted Butter
- 1 t Prepared Horseradish
- 1/2 t Dijon Mustard

1. Cook Peas in saucepan according to the package directions.
2. Drain excess water and mix with remaining ingredients over low heat until combined and warmed through.

Lemon Butter Broccoli

SERVES 4

- 2 T Unsalted Butter
- 1/4 C Lemon Juice
- 1 t Lemon Zest (optional)
- 1/8 t Tabasco/Hot Sauce
- 1/2 t Salt
- 3 C Frozen Broccoli

1. In a saucepan over medium heat, melt Butter.
2. Stir in Lemon Juice, Zest, Tabasco, and Salt. Add Broccoli and cook until heated through.

Olive Green Beans

SERVES 4

- 3 C Frozen Green Beans
- 1 T Olive Oil
- 10 Green/Calamata Olives, chopped
- 1 Tomato, diced
- 1/4 t Garlic Powder
- 1/4 C Pine Nuts, toasted

1. Cook Green Beans in saucepan according to the package directions.
2. Drain excess water and mix with remaining ingredients over low heat until combined and warmed through.

206

Stuffed Spicy Bell Pepper Boats

SERVES 4 - 8

- 1/2 lb. Ground Breakfast Sausage, browned and drained (optional)
- 1 1/2 C Rice, cooked
- 1/2 C Parmesan Cheese
- 1/4 t Tabasco/Hot Sauce
- 1/2 C Ranch Dressing
- 1/2 C Black Olives, chopped
- 1 15 oz. can Corn
- 4 Bell Peppers, cleaned and cut in half lengthwise

1. Preheat oven to 400°F.
2. In a mixing bowl blend together Sausage, Rice, Parmesan Cheese, Tabasco Sauce, Ranch Dressing, Olives, and Corn.
3. Take 1/8th of the mixture and fill a Pepper half. Repeat with remaining Peppers. Place in a 9"x13" baking dish and bake for 30 - 45 minutes.

MAIN DISH OR SIDE
Although we say that this dish serves 4, that is as an entree. If using these as side dishes, make with or without the sausage and serve up to 8.

Sweet Carrot Bake

SERVES 4

- 4 C Carrots (or Sweet Potatoes), peeled and chopped
- 1/2 C Sugar
- 2 Eggs, beaten
- 1/2 t Salt
- 4 T Unsalted Butter, melted
- 1/2 C Milk
- 1/2 t Vanilla Extract
- 1/2 C Brown Sugar
- 1/3 C Flour
- 3 T Unsalted Butter, softened
- 1/2 C Pecans, chopped

1. Place Carrots (or Sweet Potatoes) in a large saucepan and cover with cold water. Bring to a boil, reduce heat, and simmer for 20 minutes. Drain and pour Carrots into a greased 8" square baking dish.
2. Preheat oven to 325°F. In a mixing bowl, blend together Sugar, Eggs, Salt, melted Butter, Milk, and Vanilla until smooth. Pour over Carrots.
3. Mix together the Brown Sugar and Flour. Cut in the softened Butter with a fork or pizza cutter until the mixture is coarse. Stir in the Pecans and sprinkle on top.
4. Bake for 30 minutes or until the topping is lightly brown.

SWEET CARROTS
I love carrots! To make this recipe for 8, I double it and bake it in a 9"x13" baking dish for 45 minutes or until the topping is lightly brown. This dish is so sweet and yummy, it is almost a dessert, but the carrots make it a healthy option.

Tomatoes Provencal

SERVES 4

- 4 Tomatoes
- 3/4 C Bread Crumbs
- 2 Green Onions, minced
- 1/4 C Fresh Basil, minced
- 2 t Herbes de Provence
- 2 cloves Garlic, minced
- 1 t Salt
- 1/4 t Pepper
- 1/2 cup Parmesan Cheese
- 2 T Olive Oil

1. Preheat oven to 400°F.
2. Spray a 9"x13" baking dish with Non-Stick Spray.
3. Remove stem ends from Tomatoes and cut them in half crosswise. Gently core interior with a spoon.
4. Lay end down in baking dish. Mix together Bread Crumbs, Green Onions, Basil, Herbes de Provence, Garlic, Salt, Pepper, and Parmesan Cheese.
5. Sprinkle mixture over tops of each Tomato half. Drizzle with Olive Oil over tops of Tomatoes. Bake for 20 minutes or until lightly browned on top.

Desserts

BAR COOKIES
Chocolate Chip Almond Bars (p.211)
Chocolate Peppermint Bars (p.212)
White Chocolate Pecan Bars (p.213)

CAKES
Carrot Cake (p.214)
Lemon Layer Cake (p.215)
Pineapple Upside Down Cake (p.216)

CHEESECAKES
"Key" Lime Cheesecake (p.217)
Mocha Cheesecake (p.218)
Traditional Cheesecake (p.219)

CHOCOLATE
Chocolate Mousse (p.220)
Chocolate Truffles (p.221)
Hot Chocolate (p.222)

COOKIE SANDWICHES
Brownie Cookie Sandwich (p.223)
PB&J Ice Cream Sandwich (p.224)
Sugar Cookies Sandwich (p.225)

FRUIT BARS
Lemon Bars (p.226)
Margarita Bars (p.227)
Raspberry Almond Bars (p.228)

FRUIT CRISP
Apple Crisp (p.229)
Ginger Pear Crisp (p.230)

ICE CREAM AND BROWNIES
Almond Ice Cream (Pistachio) (p.231)
Coffee Ice Cream (p.232)
Cookie Dough Ice Cream (p.232)
Peanut Butter Ice Cream (p.233)
Peppermint Ice Cream (p.233)
Balsamic Raspberry Sundae (p.234)
Caramel Brownie Sundae (p.235)
Hot Fudge Brownie Sundae (p.236)
Peanut Butter Brownie Sundae (p.236)
Brownie Ice Cream Pie (p.237)

PUDDINGS
Rice Pudding (p.238)
Sandwich Bread Pudding (p.239)

PUFF PASTRY
Apple Pie Bites (p.240)
Apricot Almond Bites (p.241)
Pecan Pie Bites (p.241)
Puff Pastry Triangles (p.242)
Raspberry Cheesecakes Bites (p.243)

TARTS
Mandarin Orange Cream Tart (p.244)
Peanut Butter Tart (p.245)

WHIPPED CREAM (p.246)

pb&j ice cream sandwiches

chocolate truffles

lemon bars

mandarin orange tart

maple pecan rice pudding

traditional cheesecake

BAR COOKIES
These cookie bars are a great alternative to your standard cookies and so decadent you can eat them with a fork.

Chocolate Chip Almond Bars

MAKES 24

- 4 Eggs
- 2 C Sugar
- 1/8 t Salt
- 2 C Flour
- 2 sticks Unsalted Butter, melted
- 2 t Almond Extract
- 1/2 C Almonds, sliced or chopped
- 12 oz. Chocolate Chips

1. Preheat oven to 325°F.
2. In a mixing bowl, beat together Eggs, Sugar, and Salt with an electric hand mixer until the yolks of the Eggs turn much lighter yellow.
3. Alternate mixing in Flour and melted Butter until combined. Add Extract and beat until smooth. Fold in Almonds and Chocolate Chips.
4. Pour into a greased 9"x13" baking dish. Bake for 35-40 minutes or until very light golden. Cool before cutting.

APPLESAUCE
To cut down on the fat and calories in these Bar Cookies, try substituting 1/2 cup of applesauce for one of the sticks of butter. In fact you can generally use applesauce as a substitute for half of the oil or butter in baked dessert recipes to cut fat and calories without sacrificing a moist and delicious result.

212

Chocolate Peppermint Bars

MAKES 24

- 4 Eggs
- 2 C Sugar
- 1/8 t Salt
- 2 C Flour
- 2/3 C Cocoa Powder
- 2 sticks Unsalted Butter, melted
- 2 t Peppermint Extract
- 12 oz. White Chocolate Chips

1. Preheat oven to 325°F.
2. In a mixing bowl, beat together Eggs, Sugar, and Salt with an electric hand mixer until the yolks of the Eggs turn much lighter yellow.
3. In a separate bowl, mix Flour and Cocoa Powder together. Alternate mixing in the Flour Cocoa Powder mixture and melted Butter into the Egg mixture until combined. Add Extract and beat until smooth. Fold in White Chocolate Chips.
4. Pour into a greased 9"x13" baking dish. Bake for 35-40 minutes or until very light golden. Cool before cutting.

White Chocolate Pecan Bars

MAKES 24

- 4 Eggs
- 2 C Sugar
- 1/8 t Salt
- 2 C Flour
- 2 sticks Unsalted Butter, melted
- 2 t Vanilla Extract
- 1 C White Chocolate Chips
- 1/2 C Dried Cranberries, chopped
- 1/2 C Pecans, chopped

1. Preheat oven to 325°F.
2. In a mixing bowl, beat together Eggs, Sugar, and Salt with an electric hand mixer until the yolks of the Eggs turn much lighter yellow.
3. Alternate mixing in Flour and melted Butter until combined. Add Extract and beat until smooth. Fold in White Chocolate Chips, Dried Cranberries, and Pecans.
4. Pour into a greased 9"x13" baking dish. Bake for 35-40 minutes or until very light golden. Cool before cutting.

CAKES

Your guests will be shocked that these cakes aren't made from scratch. Because they all start with a yellow cake mix, it limits the potential for mistakes, and you always end up with a moist and delicious dessert.

Carrot Cake

SERVES 8

- 1 Yellow Cake Mix
- 3 C Carrots, grated
- 1 C Sour Cream/Plain Yogurt
- 1/3 C Vegetable Oil
- 3 Eggs
- 1 T Pumpkin Pie Spice
- 1/2 C Pineapple Chunks, with juice
- 1/3 C Raisins, optional
- 1/3 C Pecans, finely chopped, optional

CREAM CHEESE FROSTING
- 8 oz. Cream Cheese
- 2 t Vanilla
- 2 C Powdered Sugar, sifted through strainer
- 2 T Milk

1. Preheat the oven to 350°F.
2. Prepare two 9" round cake pans by spraying with Non-Stick Spray and cutting Parchment Paper into circles that fit into the bottoms.
3. Combine all ingredients in large mixing bowl and mix on low speed with hand mixer just until moistened.
4. Pour evenly into prepared pans. Bake for 30 – 35 minutes or until cake pulls away from sides and is set in the middle.
5. Allow cakes to cool.
6. Blend CREAM CHEESE FROSTING ingredients together with an electric hand mixer. (Add a little more Milk if needed to get to a spreadable texture.) Frost cooled cakes.

Lemon Layer Cake

SERVES 8

- 1 Yellow Cake Mix
- 1 C Sour Cream or Plain Yogurt
- 1/3 C Vegetable Oil
- 1/4 C Water
- 1/4 C Sugar
- 4 Eggs
- 1 T Lemon Juice
- 1 C Raspberry Jam/Jelly

LEMON GLAZE
- 2/3 C Powdered Sugar
- 2 T Lemon Juice
- 1 t Lemon Zest

1. Preheat oven to 350°F. Grease two 9" round cake pans.
2. Mix together Cake Mix, Sour Cream/Plain Yogurt, Oil, Water, Sugar, Eggs, and 1 T of Lemon Juice. Pour mix evenly into cake pans.
3. Bake for 25 - 30 minutes or until cake pulls away from sides and is set in the middle. Remove cake from pans and allow to cool.
4. In meantime Mix LEMON GLAZE ingredients together. When cakes are cool, lay one cake down on serving plate, spread with Raspberry Jam, and top with remaining cake.
5. Drizzle LEMON GLAZE over top. Garnish with Lemon slices dipped in Sugar.

CUPCAKES!
We love cupcakes, not only because they are a huge dessert trend, but also because they make cakes more versatile. (You can make one batch, and serve them for multiple events.) To make our Carrot or Lemon Cakes into cupcakes, simply spoon cake batter evenly into 24 lined muffin tins. Bake for 20 - 25 minutes and frost. (Omit raspberry jam/jelly from Lemon Cake recipe when making cupcakes.)

216

Pineapple Upside-Down Cake

SERVES 8

- 1 15 oz. can Pineapple
- 1/2 C Brown Sugar
- 1/2 C Pecans, finely chopped
- 1 Yellow Cake Mix
- 3 Eggs
- 1/2 C Unsalted Butter, melted
- 2 T Ginger

1. Preheat oven to 325°F. Grease a 8" square baking dish.
2. Drain Pineapple, reserving 2/3 C juice into a mixing bowl. Chop remaining Pineapple.
3. Sprinkle bottom of pan with Brown Sugar, Pecans, and chopped Pineapple.
4. Mix Pineapple Juice with Yellow Cake Mix, Eggs, Butter, and Ginger in a mixing bowl. Spread over toppings.
5. Bake for 55-60 minutes or until cake begins to pull away from edges and is set in the middle.
6. Let cool for 5 - 10 minutes and invert onto a serving platter.

CHEESECAKES

By using a yellow cake or brownie mix as the base, these Cheesecakes are a snap. We like to completely cool and chill Cheesecake before serving.

"Key" Lime Cheesecake

SERVES 8

- 1 Yellow Cake Mix
- 2 T Vegetable Oil
- 1 Egg
- 2 8 oz. pkgs. of Cream Cheese
- 3/4 C Sugar
- 3 Eggs
- 1 1/2 C Milk
- 1/2 C Lime Juice

1. Preheat oven to 350°F.
2. Take 1 cup of Cake Mix and reserve. Mix together the remaining Cake Mix with Vegetable Oil and 1 Egg. Press into the bottom of a greased 9" springform pan.
3. Blend together Cream Cheese and Sugar with an electric hand mixer. Add Eggs and mix well. Add remaining ingredients and blend until smooth.
4. Pour over crust. Bake for 1 hour and 15 minutes or until center is set.
5. Cool to room temperature and then chill in refrigerator.

DESSERT SAUCES

Make these Cheesecakes even more decadent by topping them with one of our Ice Cream Sundae Sauces.
Try:

Traditional Cheesecake with Caramel Sauce
Mocha Cheesecake with Peanut Butter Sauce
Key Lime Cheesecake with Balsamic Raspberry Sauce

218

Mocha Cheesecake

SERVES 8

- 1 Brownie Mix
- 2 T Vegetable Oil
- 1 Egg
- 2 8 oz. pkgs. Cream Cheese
- 1/2 C Sugar
- 3 Eggs
- 1 1/2 C Milk
- 1 C Chocolate Chips, melted
- 1/4 C Coffee, brewed (optional)

1. Preheat oven to 350°F.
2. Take 1 cup of Brownie Mix and reserve. Mix together the remaining Brownie Mix with Vegetable Oil and 1 Egg. Press into the bottom of a greased 9" springform pan.
3. Blend together Cream Cheese and Sugar with an electric hand mixer. Add Eggs and mix well. Add remaining ingredients and blend until smooth.
4. Pour over crust. Bake for 1 hour and 15 minutes or until center is set.
5. Cool to room temperature and then chill in refrigerator.

Traditional Cheesecake SK

SERVES 8

- 1 Yellow Cake Mix
- 2 T Vegetable Oil
- 1 Egg
- 2 8 oz. pkgs. Cream Cheese
- 1/2 C Sugar
- 3 Eggs
- 1 1/2 C Milk
- 3 T Lemon Juice
- 1 T Vanilla

1. Preheat oven to 350°F.
2. Take 1 cup of Cake Mix and reserve. Mix together the remaining Cake Mix with Vegetable Oil and 1 Egg. Press into the bottom of a greased 9" springform pan.
3. Blend together Cream Cheese and Sugar with an electric hand mixer. Add Eggs and mix well. Add remaining ingredients and blend until smooth.
4. Pour over crust. Bake for 1 hour and 15 minutes or until center is set.
5. Cool to room temperature and then chill in refrigerator.

CHOCOLATE
Yep! It get its own section! Enjoy!

Chocolate Mousse

SERVES 4

- 1 1/4 C Heavy/Whipping Cream, chilled
- 1/4 t Almond Extract or Cinnamon (optional)
- 1/2 C Chocolate Chips, White or Semi-Sweet

1. Place a mixing bowl in freezer.
2. Heat 1/4 C Cream in saucepan over medium heat. As edges begin to bubble, remove from heat and stir in Almond Extract or Cinnamon.
3. Add Chocolate Chips and whisk until melted and thoroughly mixed.
4. Using electric hand mixer, beat remaining cream in chilled mixing bowl until soft peaks form. Lightly fold (1/4 at a time) Chocolate into whipped Cream mixture until the chocolate is mixed in.
5. Spoon into individual cups or keep Mousse in mixing bowl. Chill for at least 1 hour.

Chocolate Truffles SK

MAKES 12

- 2 C Chocolate Chips
- 3/4 C Heavy/Whipping Cream
- 2 T Unsalted Butter
- 1 T Coffee, brewed (optional)
- 1/4 C Cocoa Powder, Powdered Sugar, and/or Chili Powder

1. Place Chocolate Chips in a mixing bowl. Heat Cream, Butter, and Coffee in a saucepan just until it starts to boil. Pour Cream mixture over Chocolate Chips in small mixing bowl. Mix until smooth.
2. Chill for 30 minutes in refrigerator.
3. With a spoon, scoop mixture out of bowl and roll into a ball with your hands. This gets messy. Do not overwork the Chocolate, or it will melt in your hands.
4. Roll ball around lightly in Cocoa Powder, Powdered Sugar, and/or Chili Powder. Keep chilled.

CHOCOLATE GANACHE

The reason these Truffles can become so melted and messy is that they are actually hardened Ganache. Keeping them chilled and not overworking them is the best way to keep them intact. Luckily they are ALWAYS delicious!

Ganache can be an excellent recipe to keep in your back pocket for dipping strawberries or frosting a cake. Simply follow the directions above, but instead of chilling, dip strawberries or drizzle over cakes while still warm. YUM YUM YUM!

222

Hot Chocolate

SERVES 2 - 4

- 3 C Milk
- 1/4 C Cocoa Powder
- 1/4 C Sugar
- 1/4 C Milk or Heavy/Whipping Cream

1. Heat 3 cups of Milk in a saucepan to desired temperature.
2. In a bowl, mix together Cocoa Powder and Sugar. Add 1/2 C Milk or Cream to create a paste.
3. Remove saucepan from heat and mix Cocoa Powder paste into warm Milk until completely dissolved. Try topped with our Whipped Cream recipe.

HOT COCOA BAR

For winter parties, we love to set up a Hot Cocoa Bar. We pour Hot Cocoa into a carafe or thermos, and lay out yummy "toppings" around it in small bowls. These "toppings" have included, candy canes, marshmallows, our Whipped Cream recipe, liquors, sprinkles, or whatever we may have available. It is fun, delicious, and an unexpected treat.

COOKIE SANDWICHES

A childhood favorite worthy of an adult soirée! Make the cookies slightly smaller to yield more sandwiches. These cookies are so good they can even be served without the filling.

Brownie Cookie Sandwich SK

MAKES 12

- 1 Brownie Mix
- 1 Egg
- 2 T Water
- 1/2 C Vegetable Oil

BUTTERCREAM
- 1/2 C Unsalted Butter, softened
- 1/2 t Vanilla Extract
- 2 C Powdered Sugar, sifted through strainer
- 1 T Milk

1. Preheat oven to 375°F.
2. Mix first 4 ingredients until moistened.
3. Drop 1 T of batter onto Parchment Paper lined jelly roll pan.
4. Bake for 7 to 8 minutes until set in center. Cool for 1 minute and then place on cooling rack to cool completely.
5. Meanwhile, blend BUTTERCREAM ingredients well with an electric hand mixer. Add a little more Milk if needed to get a spreadable texture.
6. To make sandwiches, scoop 1 - 2 tablespoons of BUTTERCREAM and sandwich between two cookies.

PB&J Ice Cream Sandwich

MAKES 12

- 1 C Unsalted Butter
- 1 C Peanut Butter
- 1 C Brown Sugar
- 1 C Sugar
- 2 Eggs
- 1 t Vanilla Extract
- 1/2 t Salt
- 2 t Baking Soda
- 2 C Flour
- 1 C Dried Cranberries or Chocolate Chips
- 2 C Vanilla Ice Cream, softened
- Pecans and Chocolate Chips, chopped (optional)

1. Preheat oven to 350°F. In a mixing bowl with an electric hand mixer, cream together Butter, Peanut Butter, and Sugar. Add Eggs and Vanilla Extract.
2. Mix together Baking Soda, Salt, and Flour.
3. Mix all together. Fold in Dried Cranberries or Chocolate Chips. Drop 1-2 tablespoons of cookie dough on a Parchment Paper covered jelly roll pan.
4. Bake cookies for approximately 10 - 12 minutes or until center is set. Cool cookies completely on cooling rack.
5. To make sandwiches, scoop 1 - 2 T of Vanilla Ice Cream and sandwich between two cookies. Roll Sides in chopped Pecans and Chocolate Chips.

Sugar Cookie Sandwich

MAKES 18

- 1 C Unsalted Butter
- 1 C Sugar
- 1 C Milk
- 2 Eggs
- 1/2 t Vanilla Extract
- 1 1/2 t Baking Powder
- 1 t Baking Soda
- 1 t Salt
- 3 1/4 C Flour
- 1/4 t Cinnamon (optional)
- Sugar (for sprinkling)

CHOCOLATE BUTTERCREAM
- 1/2 C Unsalted Butter
- 1/2 t Vanilla Extract
- 1/4 C Cocoa Powder
- 2 C Powdered Sugar, sifted through strainer
- 2 T Milk

1. Preheat oven to 350°F. In a mixing bowl with an electric hand mixer, cream together Butter and Sugar. Add Milk, Eggs, and Vanilla Extract.
2. Mix together Baking Powder, Baking Soda, Salt, Flour, and Cinnamon.
3. Mix all together. Drop 1-2 tablespoons of cookie dough on a Parchment Paper covered jelly roll pan.
4. Bake cookies for approximately 10 - 12 minutes or until center is set. Sprinkle with additional Sugar after removing from oven. Cool cookies completely on cooling rack.
1. Meanwhile, blend CHOCOLATE BUTTERCREAM ingredients with an electric hand mixer. Add a little more milk if needed to get a spreadable texture.
2. To make sandwiches, scoop 2 tablespoons of CHOCOLATE BUTTERCREAM and sandwich between two cookies.

FRUIT BARS

These bars are tangy, light, and perfect for summer, although we enjoy them all year round! Make sure they are cool before sprinkling with powdered sugar; otherwise, the sugar will melt into the bars.

Lemon Bars

MAKES 24

- 1 Yellow Cake Mix
- 1/3 C Unsalted Butter, melted
- 1 Egg, slightly beaten
- 3/4 C Lemon Juice
- 1 1/2 C Powdered Sugar
- 1/2 t Vanilla Extract
- 4 Eggs
- 2 t Lemon Zest
- 2 T Powdered Sugar (for topping)

1. Preheat the oven to 350°F. Spray a 9"x13" baking dish with Non-Stick Spray.
2. Mix together Yellow Cake Mix, Butter, and 1 Egg until crumbly and press into bottom of baking dish.
3. Bake for 20 minutes and begin to make filling. Remove from oven and turn down temperature to 300°F.
4. Mix together the Lemon Juice, 1 1/2 C of Powdered Sugar, Vanilla Extract, Eggs, and Lemon Zest and pour over partially baked crust. Bake at 300°F for 30 more minutes.
5. Take out of oven and let cool. Sprinkle, using sifter, 2 tablespoons of Powdered Sugar over cooled dessert.

Margarita Bars

MAKES 24

- 1 Yellow Cake Mix
- 1/3 C Unsalted Butter, melted
- 1 Egg, slightly beaten
- 3/4 C Lime Juice
- 1 C Mandarin Oranges, well drained and chopped
- 1 C Powdered Sugar
- 4 Eggs
- 2 T Powdered Sugar (for topping)
- 1 t Salt (optional)

1. Preheat the oven to 350°F. Spray a 9"x13" baking dish with Non-Stick Spray.
2. Mix together Yellow Cake Mix, Butter, and 1 Egg until crumbly and press into bottom of baking dish.
3. Bake for 20 minutes and begin to make filling. Remove from oven and turn down temperature to 300°F.
4. Mix together the Lime Juice, Mandarin Oranges, 1 C of Powdered Sugar, and Eggs and pour over partially baked crust. Bake at 300°F for 30 minutes.
5. Take out of oven and let cool. Sprinkle, using sifter, 2 tablespoons of Powdered Sugar and 1 teaspoon of Salt over cooled dessert.

228

Raspberry Almond Bars

MAKES 24

- 1 Yellow Cake Mix
- 1/3 C Unsalted Butter, melted
- 1 Egg, slightly beaten
- 1/2 C Raspberry Jam/Jelly
- 1/3 C Hot Water
- 1 C Powdered Sugar
- 1/2 t Almond Extract
- 4 Eggs
- 2 T Powdered Sugar (for topping)

1. Preheat the oven to 350°F. Spray a 9"x13" baking dish with Non-Stick Spray.
2. Mix together Yellow Cake Mix, Butter, and 1 Egg until crumbly and press into bottom of baking dish.
3. Bake for 20 minutes and begin to make filling. Remove from oven and turn down temperature to 300°F.
4. Mix together the Raspberry Jam/Jelly, Hot Water, 1 cup of Powdered Sugar, Almond Extract, and Eggs. Mixture will be a liquid.
5. Pour over partially baked crust. Bake at 300°F for 30 minutes.
6. Take out of oven and let cool. Sprinkle, using sifter, 2 tablespoons of Powdered Sugar over cooled dessert.

FRUIT CRIPS

Fruit Crisps are traditional comfort food at its best. These one pan desserts are simple and delicious.

Apple Crisp

SERVES 4

- 5 C Apples, peeled, cored, and diced
- 1/2 C Brown Sugar
- 1/2 t Pumpkin Pie Spice
- 1 1/2 C Almonds or Pecans, finely chopped
- 1/2 C Flour
- 1/4 C Unsalted Butter, melted
- 1/2 C Brown Sugar
- 1/4 t Pumpkin Pie Spice

1. Preheat oven to 375°F.
2. Mix together Apples, 1/2 C Brown Sugar, and 1/2 t Pumpkin Pie Spice. Pour mixture into a greased 8" square baking dish.
3. Mix together remaining ingredients. Sprinkle over Apple mixture. Press down and flatten.
4. Bake for 45 minutes or until bubbly and golden brown. Let cool slightly. Serve with Vanilla Ice Cream or our Whipped Cream recipe.

230

Ginger Pear Crisp

SERVES 4

- 3 15 oz. cans Pears, well drained
- 1/2 C Brown Sugar
- 1 T Ginger
- 1/2 C Dried Cranberries (optional)
- 1 1/2 C Almonds or Pecans, finely chopped
- 1/2 C Flour
- 1/4 C Unsalted Butter, melted
- 1/2 C Brown Sugar
- 1/4 t Pumpkin Pie Spice

1. Preheat oven to 375°F.
2. Mix together Pears, 1/2 C Brown Sugar, Ginger, and Dried Cranberries. Pour mixture into a greased 8" square baking dish.
3. Mix together remaining ingredients. Sprinkle over Pear mixture. Press down and flatten.
4. Bake for 30 minutes or until bubbly and golden brown. Let cool slightly. Serve with Vanilla Ice Cream or our Whipped Cream recipe.

ICE CREAM AND BROWNIES

This section provides an entire arsenal of quick and easy dessert options. Play with different combinations and enjoy!

Almond Ice Cream (Pistachio)

SERVES 4

- 2 C Vanilla Ice Cream, softened
- 1/4 t Almond Extract

- 1/4 C Almonds, chopped
- Green Food Coloring (optional)

1. Mix together ingredients well.
2. Refreeze if necessary.

SOFTENING AND REFREEZING ICE CREAM

We like to soften ice cream by allowing it to set out on the counter or microwaving it for 15 seconds at a time. If you soften it to the point that it is pliable, but not too soft, you may be able to avoid refreezing. If not, and you need to refreeze, be sure to stir Ice Cream regularly to avoid icicles.

Coffee Ice Cream SK

SERVES 4

- 1 C Coffee, brewed
- 2 C Vanilla Ice Cream, softened

1. In a saucepan, bring Coffee to a boil. Boil for 15 minutes to reduce to 1/4 C. Let cool.
2. Mix Coffee with Ice Cream.
3. Refreeze if necessary.

Cookie Dough Ice Cream

SERVES 4

- 2 T Sugar
- 2 T Brown Sugar
- 1 T Unsalted Butter
- 1/2 t Vanilla Extract
- 2 T Flour
- 1/4 C Chocolate Chips
- 2 C Vanilla Ice Cream, softened

1. Combine Sugars, Butter, Vanilla Extract, Flour, and Chocolate Chips. Stir in softened Ice Cream.
2. Refreeze if necessary.

Peanut Butter Ice Cream SK

SERVES 4

- 1/4 C Peanut Butter
- 2 Vanilla Ice Cream, softened

1. Melt Peanut Butter in a saucepan or microwave. Mix with Ice Cream.
2. Refreeze if necessary.

Peppermint Ice Cream

SERVES 4

- 1/8 t Peppermint Extract
- 2 C Vanilla Ice Cream, softened
- Red Food Coloring (optional)

1. Mix together ingredients well.
2. Refreeze if necessary.

234

Balsamic Raspberry Sundae

SERVES 4

BALSAMIC RASPBERRY SAUCE
- 1/2 C Raspberry Jam/Jelly
- 2 T Balsamic Vinegar
- 1 T Sugar
- 1 T Unsalted Butter

- 4 Brownies (optional)
- 2 C Vanilla Ice Cream, softened (or desired Ice Cream recipe from above)
- 1/2 C Pine Nuts, toasted (optional)

1. Combine Raspberry Jam/Jelly, Balsamic Vinegar, Sugar, and Butter in a saucepan over medium heat and cook until mixture has a syrup consistency.
2. Place Brownies in four small bowls. Top with a scoop of Ice Cream. Drizzle with BALSAMIC RASPBERRY SAUCE and sprinkle with toasted Pine Nuts.

PLAYING IT BY EAR
We love these sundaes. They are especially great to have available when you aren't sure if guests will be staying for dessert or not. We make the brownies and sauce ahead of time, and then assemble the sundaes if they decide on staying.

Caramel Brownie Sundae

SERVES 4

CARAMEL SAUCE
- 2/3 C Brown Sugar
- 2/3 C Sugar
- 1/4 C Honey
- 4 T Unsalted Butter
- 1 C Heavy/Whipping Cream

- 4 Brownies (optional)
- 2 C Vanilla Ice Cream, softened (or desired Ice Cream recipe from above)
- 1/2 C Pecans, chopped (optional)

1. To make CARAMEL SAUCE, combine Sugars and Honey in a saucepan over medium heat and cook until Sugars have melted and mixture begins to bubble. Remove from heat and add Butter and Cream.
2. Place Brownies in four small bowls. Top with a scoop of Ice Cream. Drizzle with CARAMEL SAUCE and sprinkle with Pecans.

Hot Fudge Brownie Sundae

SERVES 4

HOT FUDGE SAUCE
- 1 C Chocolate Chips (semi-sweet/white)
- 3/4 C Heavy/Whipping Cream
- 1 t Unsalted Butter
- 1 t Vanilla/Peppermint/Almond Extract (optional)

- 4 Brownies (optional)
- 2 C Vanilla Ice Cream, softened (or desired Ice Cream recipe from above)
- Peanuts, chopped (optional)

1. Place Chocolate Chips in a mixing bowl. In saucepan, over medium heat, warm Cream until edges begin to bubble. Pour immediately over Chocolate Chips. Whisk in Butter and Extracts until smooth.
2. Place Brownies in four small bowls. Top with a scoop of Ice Cream. Drizzle with HOT FUDGE SAUCE and sprinkle with Peanuts.

Peanut Butter Brownie Sundae

SERVES 4

PEANUT BUTTER SAUCE
- 4 T Unsalted Butter
- 1 C Brown Sugar
- 1/4 C Milk
- 1/2 C Peanut Butter
- 1/2 t Vanilla Extract

- 4 Brownies (optional)
- 2 C Vanilla Ice Cream, softened (or desired Ice Cream recipe from above)
- Chocolate Chips, chopped (optional)

1. Combine Butter, Brown Sugar, Milk, Peanut Butter, and Vanilla Extract in a saucepan over medium heat and cook until mixture has a syrup consistency.
2. Place Brownies in four small bowls. Top with a scoop of Ice Cream. Drizzle with PEANUT BUTTER SAUCE and sprinkle with Chocolate Chips.

Brownie Ice Cream Pie

SERVES 6 - 8

- Brownie Mix
- 2 C Vanilla Ice Cream, softened (or other recipe from above)

HOT FUDGE SAUCE
- 1 C Chocolate Chips (semi-sweet/white)
- 3/4 C Heavy/Whipping Cream
- 1 t Unsalted Butter
- 1 t Vanilla/Peppermint/Almond Extract (optional)

1. Preheat oven to 350°F.
2. Prepare Brownie Mix according to package directions. Spread over the bottom of a greased springform pan. Bake for 30 - 35 minutes or until center is set. Cool completely.
3. To make sauce, place Chocolate Chips in a mixing bowl. In saucepan over medium heat, warm Cream until edges begin to bubble. Pour immediately over Chocolate Chips. Whisk in Butter and Extracts until smooth.
4. Spread Ice Cream over top of cooled Brownies. Serve immediately drizzled with HOT FUDGE SAUCE, or other desired sauce. If Ice Cream is too soft, cover and place in freezer until frozen.

ICE CREAM BAR

A wonderful birthday party, graduation, or summer celebration treat is an Ice Cream Bar. In addition to making any of the above sauces available to your guests, also try:

Chocolate Chips, White Chocolate Chips, Pecans, Peanuts, Almonds, Pineapple Chunks, Mandarin Oranges, and/or our Whipped Cream Recipe.

PUDDINGS

These desserts are all about cozy comfort food and wonderful for a fall or winter dessert. Try these Puddings topped with vanilla ice cream or our Whipped Cream recipe.

Rice Pudding

SERVES 4 - 6

- 4 C Milk
- 1 C Heavy/Whipping Cream
- 1 C Rice
- 2/3 C Sugar
- 1/4 t Salt

1. Stir Milk, Cream, Rice, Sugar, and Salt in saucepan over medium high heat until sugar dissolves and mixture comes to a boil.
2. Reduce heat to medium-low and simmer until pudding is thick and Rice is tender, stirring occasionally for about 45 minutes. Serve warm.
3. For added flavor, try adding 1/2 C White Chocolate Chips or 1/4 C Maple Syrup and 1/4 C chopped Pecans while Rice Pudding is still warm.

Sandwich Bread Pudding

SERVES 8

- 10 slices Bread Loaf, crusts removed
- 3/4 C Raspberry Jam/Jelly, Apricot Preserves, or Peanut Butter
- 3 C Milk
- 1 C Heavy/Whipping Cream
- 3 Eggs
- 2 C Sugar

- 2 t Vanilla Extract
- 1 C Pecans, chopped (optional)
- 1/3 C Raisins, (optional)
- 1/2 C Chocolate Chips, white or semi-sweet (optional)
- 2 T Unsalted Butter

1. Preheat oven to 375°F.
2. Make 5 sandwiches with Bread triangles by spreading with Jam/Jelly, Preserves, and/or Peanut Butter. Cut each sandwich into 4 triangles.
3. Stand up triangles in a buttered 8" square baking dish with points sticking up.
4. Whisk together Milk, Cream, Eggs, Sugar and Vanilla Extract. Pour over Bread. Sprinkle with optional toppings if desired. Top Bread spikes with dollops of Butter.
5. Let bread soak for 10 – 15 minutes. Bake for 45 minutes or until center is set. Serve warm or at room temperature.

HEAVY CREAM ALTERNATIVE

Although we love having heavy cream on our list, it does spoil fairly quickly. We try to provide an alternative when possible. In the case of these puddings, try using melted vanilla ice cream instead. Just be sure to use only half of the sugar. Enjoy!

PUFF PASTRY BITES

Puff pastry is a wonderfully versatile ingredient. We love the Puff Pastry Bites below as impressive individual bite size desserts. The Puff Pastry Triangles are wonderful garnishes for Ice Cream Sundaes!

Apple Pie Bites SK

MAKES 24

- 1 sheet Puff Pastry
- 1/2 C Applesauce
- 1/4 t Cinnamon
- 3 T Brown Sugar
- 2 T Pecans, finely chopped

1. Thaw a sheet of Puff Pastry and roll out on a floured surface to approximately 11"x14".
2. With a pizza cutter, cut sheet into 24 pieces (4 rows & 6 columns). Stretch pastry squares slightly and lay into cups of a mini muffin pan.
3. Mix together Applesauce, Cinnamon, Brown Sugar, and Pecans. Fill cups with 1 teaspoon of mixture.
4. Bake at 400°F for 12 - 15 minutes or until corners begin to brown.

Apricot Almond Bites

MAKES 24

- 1/2 C Apricot Preserves
- 1/2 t Almond Extract
- 24 Almonds

1. Preheat oven to 400°F. Thaw a sheet of Puff Pastry and roll out on a floured surface to approximately 11"x14".
2. With a pizza cutter, cut sheet into 24 pieces (4 rows & 6 columns). Stretch pastry squares slightly and lay into cups of a mini muffin pan.
3. Mix together Apricot Preserves and Almond Extract. Fill Puff Pastry cups with 1 teaspoon of mixture. Top each cup with one Almond.
4. Bake for 12 - 15 minutes or until corners begin to brown.

Pecan Pie Bites SK

MAKES 24

- 1 sheet Puff Pastry
- 2 T Unsalted Butter, melted
- 1/2 C Brown Sugar
- 1 Egg, lightly beaten
- 1 t Vanilla
- 24 Pecans

1. Preheat oven to 400°F. Thaw a sheet of Puff Pastry and roll out on a floured surface to approximately 11"x14".
2. With a pizza cutter, cut sheet into 24 pieces (4 rows & 6 columns). Stretch pastry squares slightly and lay into cups of a mini muffin pan.
3. Mix together Butter, Sugar, Egg, and Vanilla Extract. Fill cups with 1 teaspoon of mixture. Top each cup with one Pecan.
4. Bake for 12 - 15 minutes or until corners begin to brown.

242

Puff Pastry Triangles SK

MAKES 24

- 1/2 sheet Puff Pastry
- 1 Egg
- 1 T Milk
- 2 t Cinnamon
- 1/3 C Sugar

1. Preheat oven to 350°F.
2. Cut pastry with pizza cutter into 6 triangles. Place on Parchment Paper lined jelly roll pan. Beat Egg lightly and mix in Milk. Brush Egg over triangles.
3. Mix Sugar and Cinnamon and sprinkle over pastry.
4. Bake for 10 minutes or until golden.

EASY AND ELEGANT
A quick, yet elegant dessert is to serve these Puff Pastry Triangles with a scoop of vanilla ice cream, drizzled with one of our sundae sauces, in a martini glass.

Raspberry Cheesecake Bites SK

MAKES 24

- 1 sheet Puff Pastry
- 4 oz. Cream Cheese, softened
- 1/4 C Powdered Sugar
- 1/4 C Raspberry Jam

1. Preheat oven to 400°F. Thaw a sheet of Puff Pastry and roll out on a floured surface to approximately 11"x14".
2. With a pizza cutter, cut sheet into 24 pieces (4 rows & 6 columns). Stretch pastry squares slightly and lay into cups of a mini muffin pan.
3. Mix together Cream Cheese, Powdered Sugar, and Raspberry Jam. Fill cups with 1 teaspoon of mixture.
4. Bake for 12 - 15 minutes or until corners begin to brown.

TARTS

These tarts share our shortbread crust and a lot of flavor. Both are served chilled and make an impressive presentation.

Mandarin Orange Tart

SERVES 8

SHORTBREAD CRUST
- 1/2 C Unsalted Butter, softened
- 1/2 C Powdered Sugar
- 1 C All Purpose Flour
- 1/8 t Salt

- 10 oz. White Chocolate Chips, melted
- 1/4 C Heavy/Whipping Cream
- 1 8 oz. pkg. Cream Cheese
- 1 10 oz. can Mandarin Oranges, well drained
- 1/4 C Apricot Preserves

1. Preheat the oven to 350°F. Blend together Butter and Sugar with electric hand mixer and gradually add Flour and Salt until mixture is made up of small crumbles.
2. Press mixture onto bottom and up sides of pie plate. Prick crust all over with a fork. Bake crust for 15 - 20 minutes.
3. Beat together Chocolate Chips and Cream. Add Cream Cheese and continue to mix. Spread over crust.
4. In a saucepan, heat Apricot Preserves and Water and stir until smooth. Pour over filling and chill tart for at least one hour before serving.

Peanut Butter Tart

SERVES 8

SHORTBREAD CRUST
- 1/2 C Unsalted Butter, softened
- 1/2 C Powdered Sugar
- 1 C All Purpose Flour
- 1/8 t Salt

- 3/4 C Peanut Butter
- 1 8 oz. pkg. Cream Cheese, softened
- 1/2 C Powdered Sugar
- 2 C Vanilla Ice Cream, softened

1. Preheat the oven to 350°F. Blend together Butter and Sugar with electric hand mixer and gradually add Flour and Salt until mixture is made up of small crumbles.
2. Press mixture onto bottom and up sides of pie plate. Prick crust all over with a fork. Bake crust for 15 - 20 minutes.
3. Mix remaining ingredients together and spread over crust. Chill until firm.
4. Try serving topped with our Hot Fudge Sauce recipe.

246

Whipped Cream

SERVES 4 - 6

- 1 C Heavy/Whipping Cream
- 2 T Sugar
- 1 t Vanilla

1. Chill a mixing bowl in freezer for about 10 minutes. With an electric hand mixer, beat the Cream until soft peaks form.
2. Lightly fold in Sugar and Vanilla until incorporated. Chill before serving.

Breakfast or Brunch

BISCOTTIS
Anise and Pine Nut Biscotti (p.249)
Chocolate Cranberry Biscotti (p.250)
Ginger Pecan Biscotti (p.251)

BREAKFAST POTATOES
Hash Browns (p.252)
Home Fries (p.253)
Potato Pancakes (p.254)

CINNAMON ROLL LOAF (p.255)

CREAM CHEESE COFFEE CAKE (p.256)

EGG DISHES
Black Bean Strata (p.257)
Breakfast Burritos (p.258)
Crab and Cream Cheese Omelette (p.259)
Eggs Benedict (p.260)
Ham and Cheese Bake (p.261)
Sausage and Bell Pepper Bake (p.262)
Spinach and Red Pepper Bake (p.263)
Tomato Basil Egg White Omelette (p.264)
Western Omelette (p.265)

FRENCH TOAST BAKES
Apricot Stuffed French Toast Bake (p.266)
Cinnamon French Toast Bake (p.267)
Raspberry French Toast Bake (p.268)

LOADED PANCAKES
Apple Cinnamon Pancakes (p.269)
Pigs in a Blanket Pancakes (p.270)
Pineapple Pancakes (p.270)
Turtle Pancakes (p.271)

QUICHES
Cracker Quiche Crust (p.272)
Puff Pastry Quiche Crust (p.272)
Broccoli and Cheese Quiche (p.273)
Ham and Apple Quiche (p.274)
Mushroom Red Pepper Quiche (p.275)
Quiche Lorraine (p.276)

SCONES
Cheddar Herb Scones (p.277)
Chocolate Chip Scones (p.278)
Cinnamon Chip Scones (p.279)
Lemon Apricot Scones (p.280)

eggs benedict

anise seed and pine nut biscotti

mushroom and red pepper quiche

cinnamon roll loaf

turtle pancakes

cheddar herb scone

BISCOTTIS

"Biscotti", in Italian, is used as a general word for cookie. They are usually twice-baked and served with a cup of coffee or tea.

Anise and Pine Nut Biscotti SK

MAKES 24

- 1 pkg. Yellow Cake Mix
- 3/4 C Flour
- 1/2 C Unsalted Butter, melted and cooled
- 2 t Vanilla Extract
- 2 Eggs
- 2 T Anise Seed/Fennel Seed, crushed
- 1/4 C Pine Nuts

1. Preheat oven to 350°F. Position rack in center of oven. Place Parchment Paper over jelly roll pan.
2. Add ingredients to a large mixing bowl.
3. Blend with an electric hand mixer set on low speed until well-blended, about 2 - 3 minutes, scraping down sides of bowl. Mixture will be very thick.
4. Transfer dough to prepared jelly roll pan and with hands form two rectangles approximately 14" x 3" x 3/4" thick. Leave 3 to 4 inches between rectangles.
5. Bake 30 - 35 minutes until firm to touch. Remove from oven (leaving oven on) and cool on pan for 10 minutes.
6. Cutting on the jelly roll pan, use a sharp knife to slice each rectangle into 3/4-inch slices on the diagonal. Turn on side and return to oven.
7. Bake biscotti 10 minutes. Remove from oven and cool completely.

Chocolate Cranberry Biscotti

MAKES 24

- 1 pkg. Yellow Cake Mix
- 1/4 C Flour
- 1/2 C Unsalted Butter, melted and cooled
- 2 t Vanilla Extract
- 2 Eggs
- 1/2 C Cocoa Powder
- 1/3 C White Chocolate Chips
- 1/3 C Dried Cranberries

1. Preheat oven to 350°F. Position rack in center of oven. Place Parchment Paper over jelly roll pan.
2. In a large mixing bowl blend together Cake Mix, Flour, melted Butter, Vanilla, Eggs, and Cocoa Powder with an electric hand mixer set on low speed until well-blended, about 2 - 3 minutes. Fold in White Chocolate Chips and Cranberries. Mixture will be very thick.
3. Transfer dough to prepared jelly roll pan and with hands form two rectangles approximately 14" x 3" x 3/4" thick. Leave 3 to 4 inches between rectangles.
4. Bake 30 - 35 minutes until firm to touch. Remove from oven (leaving oven on) and cool on pan for 10 minutes.
5. Cutting on the jelly roll pan, use a sharp knife to slice each rectangle into 3/4-inch slices on the diagonal. Turn on side and return to oven.
6. Bake biscotti 10 minutes. Remove from oven and cool completely.

Ginger Pecan Biscotti SK

MAKES 24

- 1 pkg. Yellow Cake Mix
- 3/4 C Flour
- 1/2 C Unsalted Butter, melted and cooled
- 2 t Vanilla Extract
- 2 Eggs
- 2 T Ginger
- 1/3 C Pecans, chopped

1. Preheat oven to 350°F. Position rack in center of oven. Place Parchment Paper over jelly roll pan.
2. In a large mixing bowl blend together Cake Mix, Flour, melted Butter, Vanilla, Eggs, and Ginger with an electric hand mixer set on low speed until well-blended, about 2 - 3 minutes. Fold in Pecans. Mixture will be very thick.
3. Transfer dough to prepared jelly roll pan and with hands form two rectangles approximately 14" x 3" x 3/4" thick. Leave 3 to 4 inches between rectangles.
4. Bake 30 - 35 minutes, until firm to touch. Remove from oven (leaving oven on) and cool on pan for 10 minutes.
5. Cutting on the cookie sheet, use a sharp knife to slice each rectangle into 3/4-inch slices on the diagonal. Turn on side and return to oven.
6. Bake biscotti 10 minutes longer. Remove from oven and cool completely.

COFFEE TALK

Our Biscotti is easy to make and a great treat to have on hand. It stores well in a plastic container for those impromptu coffee dates. Freezing is a great option to keep it fresher longer. Only take out what you need. Set out at room temperature an hour or so before serving.

BREAKFAST POTATOES

These Breakfast Potatoes add a lot of flavor and a decidedly diner feel to any breakfast. Great for dinnertime "breakfasts."

Hash Browns

SERVES 4

- 3 - 4 large Potatoes (Russet, Yellow, or Sweet), peeled and parboiled.
- 3 T Vegetable Oil
- 2 T Unsalted Butter
- 1 t Salt
- 1/4 t Pepper

1. With food processor or hand grater, grate Potatoes and put directly in a mixing bowl. Mix with Salt and Pepper.
2. Heat half of the Oil and Butter in fry pan. Sprinkle all of the Potatoes over top. Press flat with the back of a spatula. Cook for about 10 minutes without disturbing or until bottom of Hash Browns are golden brown.
3. Scrape bottom and flip by section, adding remaining Butter and Oil as you go.
4. Cook second side until golden brown and serve.

PARBOILING POTATOES

This is an extra step, but it allows your potatoes to be tender without scorching the outside or having them take forever to cook through.

1. Cover peeled Potatoes with water in stock pot. Bring to a boil, reduce heat to low, and allow to cook for 10 minutes.
2. Drain and rinse with cold water to cool potatoes for handling.

Home Fries

SERVES 4

- 3 - 4 large Potatoes (Russet, Yellow, or Sweet), peeled and parboiled.
- 2 T Vegetable Oil
- 2 T Unsalted Butter
- 1/4 C Shallot or Onion, diced
- 1/4 Bell Pepper, diced
- 1 t Salt
- 1/4 t Pepper
- Tabasco/Hot Sauce (to taste)

1. Chop Potatoes into 1/2 inch cubes.
2. Heat Oil and 1 tablespoon of Butter in fry pan over medium heat. Add the Onion and Bell Pepper and cook until softened. Add Potatoes and press down with a spatula.
3. Cook until Potatoes are crusty on the bottom (about 10 minutes). Sprinkle with Salt and Pepper.
4. Turn Potatoes and add additional tablespoon of Butter to pan. Cook until crisp and brown. Season with Salt, Pepper, and Tabasco Sauce.

254

Potato Pancakes

SERVES 4

- 3 - 4 large Potatoes (Russet, Yellow, or Sweet), peeled
- 1/4 C Shallot or Onion
- 2 Eggs, lightly beaten
- 3 T Flour
- 2 t Salt
- 1/4 t Pepper
- 1/4 t Pumpkin Pie Spice (optional)
- 2 T Vegetable Oil
- Applesauce (optional)
- Sour Cream (optional)

1. With food processor or hand grater, grate Potatoes and put directly in a mixing bowl.
2. Grate Shallots/Onions and mix in with Potatoes. Stir in Eggs, Flour, Salt, and Pepper.
3. Heat Oil in fry pan. With 1/2 C measuring cup, pour Potato mixture into very hot Oil.
4. Fry 3 - 4 minutes per side or until golden brown.
5. Serve with Applesauce or Sour Cream.

Cinnamon Roll Loaf SK

SERVES 4 - 6

- 1 loaf Frozen Bread Dough
- 3/4 C Sugar
- 1 T Cinnamon
- 1/2 C Unsalted Butter, melted and divided

CREAM CHEESE ICING
- 2 oz. or 1/4 C Cream Cheese
- 1/4 C Powdered Sugar
- 2 T Milk

1. In a greased loaf pan, cover and set out Bread Dough overnight to thaw and rise.
2. In the morning, preheat oven to 350°F.
3. Mix Sugar and Cinnamon in a mixing bowl. Cut Bread Dough up into 1" x 1" x 1" pieces with kitchen scissors.
4. Roll the pieces of Dough in the Cinnamon mixture.
5. Back in the loaf pan, place half of the Cinnamon and Sugar covered dough pieces. Drizzle with 1/4 of the melted Butter.
6. Top with remaining Dough pieces and then pour the rest of the Butter over top. Sprinkle the remaining Sugar and Cinnamon mixture over top.
7. Bake for 40 - 45 minutes or until golden brown.
8. Let stand for 5 minutes and invert onto a serving platter.
9. To make CREAM CHEESE ICING, beat together Cream Cheese and Sugar. Add Milk to create a glaze consistency. Spread over top of loaf.

Cream Cheese Coffee Cake SK

Choose from Raspberry, Apricot, or Chocolate! Crazy good!

SERVES 8

- 2 1/3 C All Purpose Flour
- 3/4 C Sugar
- 3/4 C Unsalted Butter
- 1/2 t Baking Powder
- 1/2 t Baking Soda
- 1/4 t Salt
- 3/4 C Sour Cream/Plain Yogurt
- 1 t Almond Extract

- 1 Egg, lightly beaten
- 1 (8 oz. pkg.) Cream Cheese, softened
- 1/4 C Sugar
- 1 Egg
- 1/2 C Raspberry Jam/Jelly, Apricot Preserves, or Chocolate Chips
- 1/2 C Almonds, sliced

1. Heat oven to 350°F. Grease and flour bottom of 9" springform pan
2. In a large mixing bowl, combine Flour and 3/4 cup of Sugar and mix well.
3. With a fork or pizza cutter, cut in Butter until mixture is coarse crumbs. Reserve 1 cup of crumb mixture.
4. To the remaining crumb mixture, add Baking Powder, Baking Soda, Salt, Sour Cream, Almond Extract, and 1 Egg. Mix until just blended, and then spread batter on bottom of pan and up the sides.
5. In a small bowl, combine Cream Cheese, 1/4 cup Sugar, and 1 Egg. Blend well.
6. Pour into batter-lined pan. Carefully spoon Jam/Jelly, Preserves, or Chocolate Chips evenly over Cream Cheese mixture.
7. Sprinkle reserved crumb mixture and sliced Almonds over top.
8. Bake at 350°F for 1 hour and 10 minutes or until Cream Cheese filling is set and crust is golden brown. Cool 15 minutes and then remove sides of pan and serve.

EASY SPREAD JAM
If you are having any difficulty spreading the jelly/jam/preserves on top of the coffee cake, try microwaving them for just a few seconds. This will make them much easier to spread!

EGG DISHES

These egg dishes cover just about any flavor combination you are looking for. The Strata and Bakes provide a make-ahead option, the quiches allow you to bake your breakfast, and the rest are just delicious!

Black Bean Strata

SERVES 4

- 1 C Salsa
- 1 C Black Beans, drained and rinsed
- 10 Flour Tortillas (8" or Fajita size), cut into 1" strips
- 1 C Cheddar Cheese, grated
- 1 C Sour Cream/Plain Yogurt
- 1 C Milk
- 1/2 t Salt
- 4 Eggs, beaten
- 1/4 C Green Onions, thinly sliced

1. Spray an 8" square baking dish with Non-Stick Spray.
2. Combine Salsa and Beans in a mixing bowl. Place 1/3 of Tortilla strips in prepared dish.
3. Top with 1/3 of Cheese and about 1/2 of the Salsa mixture. Repeat procedure with 1/3 of Tortilla strips, 1/3 cup Cheese, and remaining Salsa mixture. Top with remaining Tortilla strips.
4. Whisk together Sour Cream/Plain Yogurt, Milk, Salt, and Eggs until well blended and stir in onions. Pour over Tortilla strips and sprinkle with remaining Cheese.
5. Cover and chill 8 hours or overnight.
6. Preheat oven to 350°F. Remove dish from refrigerator. Let stand at room temperature 10 minutes.
7. Cover and bake for 20 minutes. Uncover and bake an additional 15 minutes or until lightly browned.

258

Breakfast Burritos

SERVES 4

- 6 Eggs
- 1/4 t Salt
- 1/2 C Salsa
- 1/2 lb. Sausage, cooked (optional)
- 1 C Cheddar Cheese, shredded
- 4 Flour Tortillas (8" or Fajita size), or toasted Bread

1. In a bowl, beat Eggs with Salt. Begin to scramble Eggs over medium heat. Before they are completely cooked, add Salsa, Sausage, and Cheese. Heat all ingredients thoroughly.
2. Between 2 paper towels, warm Flour Tortillas in microwave. Depending on how many Tortillas are being warmed, it should only take about 15 - 30 seconds.
3. Place 1/4 of mixture on each Tortilla and wrap up like a burrito (or make a sandwich with toast). Serve with extra Salsa and Sour Cream.

SCRAMBLED EGG TIP

No need to add anything to your eggs (like milk or water) to make them delicious. What you do need for fluffy scrambled eggs is air. Whisk the eggs for a couple of minutes, allowing them to get frothy. As you cook them, make sure that you let the eggs sit for just a minute to start to set before you begin to push the eggs (with a spatula or flat wooden spoon) towards the middle. This gives you fluffy and slightly larger "curds."

Crab and Cream Cheese Omelette

MAKES 1

- 3 Eggs
- 1/4 t Salt
- Pepper (to taste)
- 1 t Olive Oil
- 1/4 C Crab Meat, imitation (chopped) or canned lump (drained)
- 1 oz. or 2 T Cream Cheese
- 1/4 t Dill Weed

1. Whisk Eggs in a mixing bowl, getting plenty of air into them so the mixture becomes fluffy. Once the eggs have become bubbly, mix in Salt and Pepper.
2. Add Olive Oil to a fry pan, heat to medium, and pour in the Egg mixture. The bottom layer of the omelette will start to cook and solidify. Pull back on edges, slightly, towards the center of the pan, and tip the pan to allow more of the liquid to run to the edge and begin to cook. Repeat this step all the way around the edge until the base layer of the omelette is cooked and firm.
3. Sprinkle in remaining ingredients.
4. Reduce heat, fold over the omelette, and cover fry pan to allow center to cook, approximately 2 - 3 minutes more.

260

Eggs Benedict SK

SERVES 4

- 4 pieces Bread, toasted and cut into a circle
- 4 slices of Ham, cut into a circle

POACHED EGGS
- 4 Eggs
- 1 t Lemon Juice
- 4 C Water
- 1/2 t Salt

HOLLANDAISE SAUCE
- 2 Egg Yolks
- 1 T Lemon Juice
- 1/4 t Salt
- 1/2 stick Unsalted Butter

1. Layer 2 circles of toasted Bread on a dinner plate. Top with Ham slices.
2. To make poached Eggs, crack Eggs into individual, small bowls. Bring a stock pot of the Water to a boil and reduce immediately to a simmer. Stir in Lemon Juice and Salt. Lower each Egg into the water gently. Cover and cook for 3 minutes. Remove from Water and place on top of Ham.
3. To make HOLLANDAISE SAUCE, place Egg Yolks, Lemon Juice, and Salt in a blender or food processor. Blend at top speed for 2 minutes. Melt Butter in a saucepan over medium heat until foaming. With blender or food processor running, pour the hot Butter in a thin stream into the Egg Yolk mixture. By the time 2/3 of the butter is in the blender, the sauce will be thick.
4. Drizzle over poached Eggs and serve.

Ham and Cheese Bake

SERVES 4

- 5 Eggs
- 3/4 C Milk
- 1 T Yellow Mustard
- 1/2 t Salt
- 1/4 t Pepper (or to taste)
- 4 slices Bread, cut into cubes
- 1 C Ham, diced
- 3/4 C Cheddar Cheese, grated

1. Grease an 8" square baking dish with Non-Stick Spray.
2. In a mixing bowl, whisk together Eggs, Milk, Mustard, Salt, and Pepper.
3. Spread Bread cubes on the bottom of baking dish. Top with Ham and then Cheese. Pour Egg mixture over top. Refrigerate overnight.
4. Preheat oven to 350°F and bake about 50 minutes or until center is puffed and set.

MAKE MORE!
These bake recipes are so easy and delicious, they are perfect for large groups. To serve 8, double the recipe and place in a 9"x13" baking dish. Bake for approximately 1 hour or until center is puffed and set.

Sausage and Bell Pepper Bake SK

SERVES 4

- 5 Eggs
- 3/4 C Milk
- 1 T Yellow Mustard
- 1/2 t Salt
- 1/4 t Pepper (or to taste)
- 4 slices Bread, cut into cubes
- 1/2 pound Ground Breakfast Sausage, cooked
- 1/4 C Bell Peppers, diced
- 1/4 C Shallots/Onions, diced
- 3/4 C Cheddar Cheese, grated

1. Grease an 8" square baking dish with Non-Stick Spray.
2. In a mixing bowl, whisk together Eggs, Milk, Mustard, Salt, and Pepper.
3. Spread Bread cubes on the bottom of baking dish. Top with Sausage, Pepper, Shallot/Onions, and then Cheese. Pour Egg mixture over top.
4. Refrigerate overnight.
5. Preheat oven to 350°F and bake about 50 minutes or until center is puffed and set.

Spinach and Red Pepper Bake

SERVES 4

- 5 Eggs
- 3/4 C Milk
- 1 T Yellow Mustard
- 1/2 t Salt
- 1/4 t Pepper (or to taste)
- 4 slices Bread, cut into cubes
- 1 C Spinach, thawed and squeezed dry
- 2 Roasted Red Peppers, diced
- 3/4 C Cheddar Cheese, grated

1. Grease an 8" square baking dish with Non-Stick Spray.
2. In a mixing bowl, whisk together Eggs, Milk, Mustard, Salt, and Pepper.
3. Spread Bread cubes on the bottom of baking dish. Top with Spinach, Roasted Red Pepper, and then Cheese. Pour Egg mixture over top.
4. Refrigerate overnight.
5. Preheat oven to 350°F and bake about 50 minutes until center is puffed and set.

DOUBLE IT!

These bake recipes are so easy and delicious, they are perfect for large groups. To serve 8, double the recipe and place in a 9"x13" baking dish. Bake for approximately 1 hour or until center is puffed and set.

264

Tomato Basil Egg White Omelette

MAKES 1

- 4 Egg Whites
- 1/4 t Salt
- Pepper (to taste)
- 1 t Olive Oil
- 1/2 Tomato, thinly sliced
- 1 T Fresh Basil, finely chopped
- 2 T Feta or Parmesan Cheese

1. Whisk Egg Whites in a mixing bowl, getting plenty of air into them so the mixture becomes fluffy. Once the Egg Whites have become bubbly, mix in Salt and Pepper.
2. Add Olive Oil to a fry pan, heat to medium, and pour in the Egg mixture. The bottom layer of the omelette will start to cook and solidify. Pull back on edges, slightly, towards the centre of the pan, and tip the pan to allow more of the liquid to run to the edge and begin to cook. Repeat this step all the way around the edge until the base layer of the omelette is cooked and beginning to firm.
3. Sprinkle in remaining ingredients.
4. Reduce heat, fold over the omelette, and cover fry pan to allow center to cook, approximately 2 - 3 minutes more.

Western Omelette

MAKES 1

- 3 Eggs
- 1/4 t Salt
- Pepper (to taste)
- 1 t Olive Oil
- 1/4 C Ham, diced
- 2 T Bell Pepper, diced
- 2 T Shallot or Onions, diced
- 1/4 C Cheddar Cheese, shredded

1. Whisk Eggs in a mixing bowl, getting plenty of air into them so the mixture becomes fluffy. Once the eggs have become bubbly, mix in Salt and Pepper.
2. Add Olive Oil to a fry pan, heat to medium, and pour in the Egg mixture. The bottom layer of the omelette will start to cook and solidify. Pull back on edges, slightly, towards the centre of the pan, and tip the pan to allow more of the liquid to run to the edge and begin to cook. Repeat this step all the way around the edge until the base layer of the omelette is cooked and beginning to firm.
3. Sprinkle in remaining ingredients.
4. Reduce heat, fold over the omelette, and cover fry pan to allow center to cook, approximately 2 - 3 minutes more.

FRENCH TOAST BAKES

These casseroles are a simple and delicious make-ahead breakfast with a bread pudding consistency. The recipe below serves four. To serve eight, double the recipe, use a 9"x13" baking dish, and bake for an hour and 10 minutes or until center is set.

Apricot Stuffed French Toast Bake

SERVES 4

- 1/2 8 oz. pkg. Cream Cheese
- 2 T Sour Cream/Plain Yogurt
- 1/4 C Apricot Preserves
- 9 slices Bread, crusts removed
- 3 Eggs
- 2 T Sugar
- 1 1/2 C Milk
- 1 t Vanilla Extract
- 2 T Sugar (additional)
- 1 t Cinnamon

1. Blend together Cream Cheese and Sour Cream/Plain Yogurt until well combined.
2. In a greased 8" square baking dish, spread about about 2 teaspoons of Preserves on one side of 3 slices of Bread. Then, spread 1/3 of Cream Cheese mixture over Preserves. Lay those, Preserves side down, into baking dish. Cut 1 slice of bread in half to best fit it in the baking dish. Continue until all Bread and fillings have been used up (3 layers total).
3. In a mixing bowl, whisk together Eggs, Sugar, Milk, and Vanilla Extract. Pour evenly over Bread. Top with mixture of 2 tablespoons of Sugar and 1 teaspoon Cinnamon.
4. Cover and refrigerate overnight or for at least 2 hours. Bake uncovered at 350°F for 1 hour. Let set for 10 minutes and serve with Maple Syrup.

Cinnamon French Toast Bake

SERVES 4

- 1/4 C Unsalted Butter, melted
- 1/2 C Brown Sugar
- 1 t Cinnamon
- 9 slices Bread, crusts removed
- 3 Eggs
- 2 T Sugar
- 1 1/2 C Milk
- 1 t Vanilla Extract
- 2 T Sugar (additional)
- 1 t Cinnamon

1. Mix together 1/4 C melted Butter, 1 t Cinnamon, and 1/2 C Brown Sugar.
2. In a greased 8" square baking dish, sprinkle 1/3 of Butter mixture on bottom of baking dish. Use three slices of Bread (one slice cut in half) and lay that Bread on top of Butter mixture. Continue until all Bread and fillings have been used up (3 layers total).
3. In a mixing bowl, whisk together Eggs, Sugar, Milk, and Vanilla Extract. Pour evenly over Bread. Top with mixture of 2 tablespoons of Sugar and remaining Cinnamon.
4. Cover and refrigerate overnight or for at least 2 hours. Bake uncovered at 350°F for 1 hour. Let set for 10 minutes and serve with Maple Syrup.

268

Raspberry French Toast Bake SK

SERVES 4

- 1/4 C Raspberry Jam/Jelly
- 1/2 C White Chocolate Chips
- 1/2 C Pecans, finely chopped
- 9 slices Bread, crusts removed
- 3 Eggs
- 2 T Sugar
- 1 1/2 C Milk
- 1 t Vanilla Extract
- 2 T Sugar (additional)
- 1 t Cinnamon

1. In a greased 8" square baking dish, sprinkle 1/3 of White Chocolate Chips and Pecans. Spread about 2 teaspoons of Jam on one side of 3 slices of Bread. Lay those, Jam/Jelly side down, into baking dish. Cut 1 slice of bread in half to best fit it in the baking dish. Continue until all Bread and fillings have been used up (3 layers total).
2. In a mixing bowl, whisk together Eggs, Sugar, Milk, and Vanilla Extract. Pour evenly over Bread. Top with mixture of 2 tablespoons of Sugar and 1 teaspoon Cinnamon.
3. Cover and refrigerate overnight or for at least 2 hours. Bake uncovered at 350°F for 1 hour. Let set for 10 minutes and serve with Maple Syrup.

LOADED PANCAKES

Take your favorite pancake mix up a few notches with these delicious and creative additions! We prefer to buy mixes that are NOT "Complete", because these mixes (that only require you to add water) limit our options. If you do use a "Complete" mix, make batter according to its package directions.

Apple Cinnamon Pancake

SERVES 4

• 1 1/2 C Pancake Mix (not "Complete")
• 3/4 C Milk
• 1 T Vegetable Oil
• 1 Egg
• 1/2 t Cinnamon
• 1 Apple, peeled, cored, and thinly sliced

1. Mix together all ingredients. Mix until just combined. Some lumps are acceptable.
2. Heat a fry pan over medium heat. Spray with Non-Stick Spray. Pour 1/4 C of pancake batter onto pan as many times as the size of pan allows. When bubbles form on the top of the entire pancake, flip and continue to cook for 1 - 2 minutes more.
3. Serve warm with Maple Syrup.

WARM MAPLE SYRUP
We like to serve warm maple syrup with these Loaded Pancakes. It is a simple step with a decadent result. Simply warm over low heat in a saucepan or microwave, in a microwave safe bowl, for 30 seconds at a time until warmed through.

Pigs in a Blanket Pancake

SERVES 4

- 1 1/2 C Pancake Mix (not "Complete")
- 3/4 C Milk
- 1 T Vegetable Oil
- 1 Egg
- 1/4 C Ground Breakfast Sausage (cooked) or Bacon (cooked and finely chopped)

1. Mix together all ingredients. Mix until just combined. Some lumps are acceptable.
2. Heat a fry pan over medium heat. Spray with Non-Stick Spray. Pour 1/4 C of pancake batter onto pan as many times as the size of pan allows. When bubbles form on the top of the entire pancake, flip and continue to cook for 1 - 2 minutes more.
3. Serve warm with Maple Syrup.

Pineapple Pancake

SERVES 4

- 1 1/2 C Pancake Mix (not "Complete")
- 3/4 C Milk
- 1 T Vegetable Oil
- 1 Egg
- 1/4 C Pineapple, well drained and finely chopped

1. Mix together all ingredients. Mix until just combined. Some lumps are acceptable.
2. Heat a fry pan over medium heat. Spray with Non-Stick Spray. Pour 1/4 C of pancake batter onto pan as many times as the size of pan allows. When bubbles form on the top of the entire pancake, flip and continue to cook for 1 - 2 minutes more.
3. Serve warm with Maple Syrup.

Turtle Pancake

SERVES 4

- 1 1/2 C Pancake Mix (not "Complete")
- 3/4 C Milk
- 1 T Vegetable Oil
- 1 Egg
- 1/4 C Chocolate Chips
- 2 T Pecans, chopped

CARAMEL SAUCE
- 2/3 C Brown Sugar
- 2/3 C Sugar
- 1/4 C Honey
- 4 T Unsalted Butter
- 1 C Heavy/Whipping Cream

1. Mix together pancake ingredients. Mix until just combined. Some lumps are acceptable.
2. Heat a fry pan over medium heat. Spray with Non-Stick Spray. Pour 1/4 C of pancake batter onto pan as many times as the size of pan allows. When bubbles form on the top of the entire pancake, flip and continue to cook for 1 - 2 minutes more.
3. To make CARAMEL SAUCE, stir together Sugars, Honey, and Butter in a saucepan over medium heat until the mixture bubbles. Remove from heat and stir in Cream. Drizzle over pancakes.

QUICHES

All of these Quiches have three crust options. Pick from Cracker Crust, crustless, or Puff Pastry.

Cracker Quiche Crust

- 1 1/2 C Butter Crackers (Approximately 35 crackers)
- 4 T Unsalted Butter, melted

1. Preheat oven to 350°F. Place crackers in a Resealable Storage Bag and crush with a rolling pin.
2. Mix Cracker crumbs and melted Butter and press firmly into bottom and up sides of a pie plate. Bake for 10 minutes.
3. Remove from oven. Pour in filling of choice. (See following pages.) Return to oven.
4. Continue to bake 45 minutes or until center has set.

Puff Pastry Quiche Crust

- 1 sheet Puff Pastry

1. Preheat oven to 400°F.
2. Thaw a sheet of Puff Pastry and roll out on a floured surface to approximately 11"x14". With a pizza cutter cut sheet into 12 pieces (3 rows & 4 columns). Stretch pastry squares slightly and lay into muffin pan cups.
3. Fill cups with 1/12th of fillings of choice. (See following pages.)
4. Bake at 400°F for 20 minutes or until corners begin to brown.

Broccoli and Cheese Quiche

SERVES 4 - 6

- 1 C Frozen Broccoli or Spinach, thawed and drained (Spinach needs to be squeezed)
- 1 C Cheddar Cheese, shredded
- 4 Eggs
- 1/2 C Milk
- 1/2 C Heavy/Whipping Cream or Sour Cream/Plain Yogurt
- 2 T Dried Minced Onions
- 1/2 t Salt
- Pepper (to taste)

1. For "crustless" quiche, preheat oven to 375°F. Otherwise, choose crust from beginning of this section and prepare accordingly.
2. Sprinkle greased pie plate or crust(s) with Broccoli or Spinach and Cheese.
3. Whisk together Eggs, Milk, Cream, Dried Minced Onions, Salt, and Pepper. Pour in Egg mixture.
4. Bake for 45 minutes or until center is set or bake according to preferred Crust option. Let stand for approximately 5 minutes and then serve.

LARGE BRUNCHES
Smaller bite size quiches are great to serve for large groups. Use any of these quiche recipes with 2 puff pastry sheets cut up to fill 48 mini-muffin cups. Use only a teaspoon of quiche mixture and bake at 400°F for 12 - 15 minutes.

274

Ham and Apple Quiche

SERVES 4 - 6

- 1 C Cheddar Cheese, shredded
- 1 C Ham, diced
- 1 Apple, peeled, cored, and grated
- 1/2 t Cinnamon
- 1/2 C Heavy/Whipping Cream or Sour Cream/Plain Yogurt
- 1/2 C Milk
- 4 Eggs
- 2 T Yellow Mustard
- 1/8 t Garlic Powder
- 1/2 t Salt

1. For "crustless" quiche, preheat oven to 375°F. Otherwise, choose crust from beginning of this section and prepare accordingly.
2. Toss together Cheeses, Ham, grated Apples, and Cinnamon. Pour into greased pie plate or crust(s).
3. Whisk together Cream, Milk, Eggs, Mustard, Garlic Powder, and Salt. Pour Egg mixture over Ham and Apple mixture.
4. Bake for 45 minutes or until center is set or bake according to preferred Crust option. Let stand for approximately 5 minutes and then serve.

Mushroom Red Pepper Quiche

SERVES 4 - 6

- 1 4 oz. can Mushrooms, drained
- 1 Roasted Red Pepper, diced
- 1/2 C Mozzarella Cheese
- 1/2 C Feta Cheese
- 1/2 C Milk
- 1/2 C Heavy/Whipping Cream or Sour Cream/Plain Yogurt
- 4 Eggs
- 1/2 t Salt
- 1/4 t Pepper

1. For "crustless" quiche, preheat oven to 375°F. Otherwise, choose crust from beginning of this section and prepare accordingly.
2. Sprinkle greased pie plate or crust(s) with Mushrooms, diced Roasted Red Pepper, and Cheeses.
3. Whisk together Eggs, Milk, Cream, Salt, and Pepper. Pour in Egg mixture.
4. Bake for 45 minutes or until center is set or bake according to preferred Crust option. Let stand for approximately 5 minutes and then serve.

276

Quiche Lorraine SK

SERVES 4 - 6

- 4 slices Bacon, cooked and crumbled
- 1/2 C Mozzarella Cheese
- 1/2 C Parmesan Cheese
- 4 Eggs
- 1/2 C Heavy/Whipping Cream or Sour Cream/Plain Yogurt
- 1/4 t Salt
- 1/8 t Pepper
- 1/8 t Nutmeg

1. For "crustless" quiche, preheat oven to 375°F. Otherwise, choose crust from beginning of this section and prepare accordingly.
2. Sprinkle greased pie plate or crust(s) with Bacon and Cheeses.
3. Whisk together Eggs, Milk, Cream, Salt, Pepper, and Nutmeg. Pour in Egg mixture.
4. Bake for 45 minutes or until center is set or bake according to preferred Crust option. Let stand for approximately 5 minutes and then serve.

SCONES

These scone recipes are flakey and delicious. Try them for breakfast, brunch, or anytime.

Cheddar Herb Scones

MAKES 12

- 1 3/4 C Flour
- 4 t Baking Powder
- 1 T Sugar
- 1/2 t Salt
- 5 T Unsalted Butter, cold and cut into pieces
- 1/3 C Milk
- 1/4 C Sour Cream/Plain Yogurt
- 1/2 C Cheddar Cheese, shredded
- 1 t Herbes de Provence

1. Preheat the oven to 400°F.
2. Sift the Flour, Baking Powder, Sugar, and Salt into a mixing bowl. Cut Butter into mixture, using a pizza cutter or fork, until mixture is crumbly.
3. Mix Milk and Sour Cream/Plain Yogurt into Butter/Flour mixture. Stir just until combined. Fold in Herbes de Provence and Cheese.
4. Roll into 2 inch balls and place on a Parchment Paper covered jelly roll pan, about 2 inches apart, and flatten lightly.
5. Bake for 10 to 15 minutes or until golden brown.

278

Chocolate Chip Scones

MAKES 12

- 1 3/4 C Flour
- 4 t Baking Powder
- 1/3 C White Sugar
- 1/8 t Salt
- 5 T Unsalted Butter, cold and cut into pieces
- 1/3 C Milk
- 1/4 C Sour Cream/Plain Yogurt
- 1 t Vanilla Extract
- 1/2 C Chocolate Chips

1. Preheat the oven to 400°F.
2. Sift the Flour, Baking Powder, Sugar, and Salt into a mixing bowl. Cut Butter into mixture, using a pizza cutter or fork, until mixture is crumbly.
3. Mix Milk and Sour Cream/Plain Yogurt, and Vanilla Extract into Butter/Flour mixture. Stir just until combined. Fold in Chocolate Chips.
4. Roll into 2 inch balls and place on a Parchment Paper covered jelly roll pan, about 2 inches apart, and flatten lightly.
5. Bake for 10 to 15 minutes or until golden brown.

Cinnamon Chip Scones SK

MAKES 12

CINNAMON CHIPS
- 3 T Sugar
- 1 T Cinnamon
- 2 t Unsalted Butter
- 2 t Honey

- 1 3/4 C Flour
- 4 t Baking Powder
- 1/3 C White Sugar
- 1/8 t Salt
- 5 T Unsalted Butter, cold and cut into pieces
- 1/3 C Milk
- 1/4 C Sour Cream/Plain Yogurt
- 1 t Vanilla Extract

1. To make CINNAMON CHIPS, preheat oven to 250°F. In a large bowl, combine the Sugar, Cinnamon, Butter, and Honey with a fork until crumbly and evenly blended. Spread onto an Aluminum Foil lined baking sheet. Bake at 250° for 30-40 minutes or until melted and bubbly. Cool completely; break into small pieces.
2. Preheat the oven to 400°F. Sift the Flour, Baking Powder, Sugar, and Salt into a mixing bowl. Cut Butter into mixture, using a pizza cutter, until mixture is crumbly.
3. Mix Milk, Sour Cream/Plain Yogurt, and Vanilla Extract into Butter/Flour mixture. Stir just until combined. Fold in CINNAMON CHIPS.
4. Roll into 2 inch balls and place on a Parchment Paper covered jelly roll pan, about 2 inches apart, and flatten lightly.
5. Bake for 10 to 15 minutes or until golden brown.

SAVE A STEP
These Cinnamon Chips are super good; however, if you don't have time to take that extra step, just add the 3 T sugar and 1 T cinnamon to scone batter. They will still be cinnalicious!

280

Lemon Apricot Scones

MAKES 12

- 2 1/4 C Flour
- 4 t Baking Powder
- 1/2 C Sugar
- 1/8 t Salt
- 6 T Unsalted Butter, cold and cut into pieces
- 1/3 C Lemon Juice
- 2 t Lemon Zest
- 1/2 C Sour Cream/Plain Yogurt
- 1/4 C Apricot Preserves

1. Preheat the oven to 400°F.
2. Sift the Flour, Baking Powder, Sugar, and Salt into a mixing bowl. Cut Butter into mixture, using a pizza cutter, until mixture is crumbly.
3. Mix Lemon Juice, Lemon Zest, Apricot Preserves, and Sour Cream/Plain Yogurt into Butter/Flour mixture. Stir just until combined.
4. Roll into 2 inch balls and place on a Parchment Paper covered jelly roll pan, about 2 inches apart, and flatten lightly.
5. Bake for 10 to 15 minutes or until golden brown.

Glossary

8" Square Baking Dish - glass or metal dish with 8" square base and approximately 3 inch sides. We prefer glass for its presentation.

9" Round Cake Pans - metal (often aluminum) pans with a 9" diameter, and approximately 1.5" tall sides. It is best to have at least two.

9"x13" Baking Dish - glass or metal dish with 9" x 13" base and approximately 3 inch sides. We prefer glass for its presentation.

Aluminum Foil - thin, pliable, metal sheets made from aluminum. Great for wrapping food and reducing the clean-up on baking pans.

Anise Seed/Fennel Seed - seeds from respective plants that smell and taste similar to licorice. Fennel seed is more aromatic and a bit sweeter. In addition to its use in savory dishes, Anise seed is found more often in Italian desserts and liquors.

Applesauce - a puree made from cooked and mashed apples. Generally found by the canned fruit. Substitute applesauce instead of half the oil in any sweet baked good recipe to reduce calories and fat. We prefer to buy unsweetened in 4 ounce cups to maintain freshness longer. Four ounces is about 1/2 of a cup.

Apples (fresh) - cored fruit available in many colors and varieties. We like Fuji and Gala apples for their flavor and versatility. Keep apples in the refrigerator. Apples do not freeze well.

Apricot Preserves - apricots cooked in sugar to preserve them. Found by the jams and jellies. Both jam and preserves contain actual fruit, however, jam is made from fruit pulp or crushed fruit, while preserves are comprised of fruit chunks.

Artichoke Hearts, marinated (jar) - hearts of the artichoke marinated in oil, vinegar, salt, and spices. Generally found by the canned vegetables. Some brands have more oil in their marinated versions which equals more calories and fat without a lot of added flavor.

Bacon - side, belly, or back cut of pork that has been cured, smoked, or both. Bacon is available in regular or thick cut versions. We prefer the regular cuts for Bacon Wraps.

Baking Powder - leavening agent of sodium bicarbonate, cream of tartar, and starch. In general you use baking powder when there is no acidity in the recipe like buttermilk, chocolate, or honey. It works like yeast, but much faster. It is available in non-alum and found in the baking section of most grocers. Best if kept in the refrigerator (make sure it is air-tight).

Baking Soda - leavening agent of sodium bicarbonate. Found in the baking section of most grocers. Store in a resealable storage bag or air-tight plastic container in your fridge.

Barbecue Sauce - sauce generally made of tomato puree, onions, sugar, and vinegar. Found near other condiments, like ketchup, in most grocers.

Basil, fresh - green leafed herb. To keep basil fresh longer, keep it in the refrigerator, wrapped in a damp paper towel, and in a resealable storage bag. Growing your own basil is another great option.

Beans, Black (can) - small beans with a glossy black shell canned in water and salt in a thick syrupy liquid. After draining and rinsing black beans, they can be used in salads, nachos, and wraps without cooking.

Beans, Kidney (can) - a larger, kidney shaped bean with a, generally, reddish hue and canned in a thick syrupy liquid. They come in light and dark varieties. Dark varieties have a slightly thicker and tougher skin.

Beans, Northern/Cannellini (can) - white beans that can be used interchangeably. Northern Beans have a bit of a powdery texture. Cannellini beans are actually thin skinned white kidney beans. Use either to substitute for garbanzo beans (chick peas).

Bell Pepper, Red or Green (fresh)- sweet fleshed bell shaped pepper. The different colors of bell peppers show the different stages of ripeness. Green peppers are actually "unripe" and red peppers are fully ripe. Yellow and orange are in between. In turn, red peppers will be the sweetest while green are the least sweet and most bitter tasting. What is kept on hand is your personal preference. Store unwashed in a plastic bag in your refrigerator.

Bread Crumbs, plain - crumbs of dried bread. Panko are a style of coarse Japanese bread crumbs that can be substituted. Store in an airtight container in a pantry or refrigerator.

> To substitute Italian bread crumbs add 1/4 t of garlic powder and 1 T of Italian seasonings per 1 C of bread crumbs.

> To make quick homemade breadcrumbs, remove crusts from bread and place at 300°F in the oven on a jelly roll pan. Bake until slightly browned, approximately 10-15 minutes Let bread cool and pulse in food processor.

Bread Dough (frozen) - loaf of raw frozen bread dough. Found bagged in freezer section of most grocers.

Bread Loaf, white or wheat - loaf of white or wheat sliced bread. Can be frozen to extend shelf life.

Broccoli (frozen) - green vegetable from the cabbage family. Found in the frozen foods section. See package cooking directions.

Broth, Beef (can) - liquid made from simmering beef and vegetables. Substitute for water in beef or tomato based soups, chilis, and stews to make them taste like they've been simmering all day. If purchasing larger packages of broth than recommended, a good rule of thumb is that a 15 oz. can equals approximately 2 cups.

Broth, Chicken (can) - liquid from simmering chicken and vegetables. Substitute for water in chicken, seafood, or green vegetable based soups, chilis, and stews to make them taste like they've been simmering all day. Use to cook pasta or rice for extra richness and flavor. If purchasing larger packages of broth than recommended, a good rule of thumb is that a 15 oz. can equals approximately 2 cups.

Brownie Mix - a prepackaged brownie mix generally made from sugar, flour, vanilla extract, and cocoa powder. Found in the baking section of most grocers. Choose any variety you would like; however, each of our recipes call for the 8" square pan size.

Butter Crackers - packaged crackers made with butter. Found in the salty snacks section of most grocers.

Butter, unsalted - made from churning fresh or fermented cream or milk. If you do use salted butter, omit 1/4 teaspoon extra salt out of the recipe for every 1/2 C of butter. Keep refrigerated. Sticks at room temperature, however, are easier to spread.

Cabbage and Carrot Mix, shredded - (Coleslaw Mix) chopped cabbage and carrots found near the bagged salads section of most grocers. It can be used for coleslaw but also in many Asian dishes, soups, and stews. Store in the refrigerator.

Cake Mix, Yellow - a prepackaged cake mix generally made from sugar, flour, leavening, salt, and powdered milk. Found in the baking section of most grocers.

Carrots (fresh) - taproot vegetables. We substitute mashed carrots for mashed sweet potatoes in casseroles. Store in a plastic bag in the refrigerator.

Celery (fresh) - slightly bitter stalked vegetable. Store in a plastic bag in fridge.

Cheese, Bleu or Gorgonzola - bleu is a group of strong and tangy cheeses known for their characteristic blue veining. We prefer to buy it crumbled. Gorgonzola is a milder Italian bleu cheese. If you do not like bleu cheese, substitute equal amounts of mozzarella or parmesan in our recipes.

Cheese, Feta - a brine cured, tangy, Greek cheese generally made from sheep's milk. We prefer to buy it crumbled. If you don't enjoy feta cheese, substitute an equal amount of parmesan or mozzarella cheese in our recipes.

Cheese, Cheddar - mild, medium, or sharp hard table cheeses. We like to buy this cheese in blocks because it provides many more uses; however, buying it pre-shredded does alleviate a step for many recipes. Can be frozen to increase shelf life.

Cheese, Mozzarella Shredded - shredded, generally low moisture, white cheese. We chose to have shredded mozzarella on hand because of its ease and versatility. Can be frozen to increase shelf life.

Cheese, Parmesan or Asiago - hard white grating cheeses. These cheeses can be purchased pre-shredded in a shaker or in chunks. When buying them in chunks, parmesan should always be purchased with a rind. It is a cheese made from raw cow's milk and has a salty, nutty flavor. Parmigiano Reggiano is a DOP (or Protected Designation of Origin) version of parmesan cheese. Asiago cheese is similar to parmesan in that it is made from cow's milk and is considered a "grating" cheese. It is sweet and buttery with less salt. If buying these cheeses in chunks, wrap in a sheet of parchment paper and then seal in a resealable storage bag in the refrigerator. If buying in large quantities, they can be frozen to add shelf life.

Chicken Breast (Boneless Skinless) - breast of chicken with bone and skin removed. Chicken can be frozen to add shelf life. Available at many grocers and warehouse stores in large bags where the chicken has been individually frozen. This is generally less expensive and allows you to only defrost and cook what you need.

Chicken Thighs (Boneless Skinless) - thigh of chicken with bone and skin removed. Because they have a higher fat content, they are a great option for baked chicken dishes to avoid having dry meat. Chicken can be frozen to add shelf life.

Chili Powder - a ground blend of dehydrated hot chili peppers and other flavors, which can include garlic, cumin, and salt. Found in spice section of most grocers, the chili powder most commonly available doesn't have a tremendous amount of heat. To retain good flavor and potency it is best to use dried spices within one year.

Chocolate Chips, semi-sweet - small drops of chocolate containing cocoa liquor, sugar, cocoa butter, and vanilla. Found in the baking section of most grocers.

Chocolate Chips, white - small drops of confection containing sugar, cocoa butter, and milk solids. Found in the baking section of most grocers.

Cinnamon, ground - ground bark of a small evergreen tree. Found in spices section of most grocers. To retain good flavor and potency, it is best to use dried spices within one year.

Cocoa Powder - made from pressed chocolate liquor to remove most of its cocoa butter. Cocoa powder is found in the baking section of most grocers and is available in regular or "dark" varieties. Dutch processed cocoa powder is treated with an alkali to neutralize its acids and has a milder taste than the natural processed cocoa. Keep in a cool, dry pantry out of sunlight.

Coffee (regular & decaf) - seeds of the coffee plant. Store coffee in an air-tight glass or plastic container in a cool, dark place.

Corn (can) - canned kernels of corn soaked in water and salt. You can substitute equal amounts of pureed corn kernels anytime you see "cream style corn."

Crab Meat, imitation/lump (plastic package or can) - imitation crab (Krab) is generally made of Alaskan Pollack and is found in the refrigerated seafood section of most grocers. Lump crab meat is real Crab from the body of the animal and is found canned near canned tunas.

Cranberries, dried - (Craisins) are dried, tart berries. Dried cranberries are generally found in fresh produce sections near raisins and are available sweetened or unsweetened. Dried cranberries should be kept in a resealable container in your pantry.

Cream Cheese - rich soft cheese made from soured cream and milk. Found in the dairy section of most grocers. We prefer to purchase in a brick form. Light cream cheese is an acceptable substitution, but we do not recommend "fat free."

Cream, Heavy or Whipping - a high fat milk product made from milk. Heavy cream has a higher fat content than whipping cream. Can be frozen to add shelf life; however, cream will not make whipped cream again after freezing.

Cucumber, English - (Hot House or Seedless) thin skinned cucumbers grown in a greenhouse. English cucumbers are the long ones found wrapped in plastic in the fresh produce section of many grocers. We like them because they have very small, soft seeds and a very thin skin, which makes peeling unnecessary. Refrigerate in plastic wrap or bag.

Cumin, ground - ground seeds of a flowering plant. Found in spice section of most grocers, cumin has a distinct and smoky taste. Cumin is found in many Southwest, Mexican, Middle Eastern, and North African dishes. To retain good flavor and potency, it is best to use dried spices within one year.

Deep Dish Pizza Pan - round metal pan for cooking pizzas with 2 - 3 inch sides.

Dill Weed - dried, chopped, dill plant. To retain good flavor and potency, it is best to use dried spices within one year.

Egg Noodles - wide flat noodles usually made from flour and egg yolks, although "yolkless" varieties are available. Egg noodles (also labeled "Wide Egg Noodles") are found by pastas in most grocers.

Eggs - chicken eggs. If eggs are bad, they will float in a pot of cold water. Keep eggs refrigerated.

Electric Hand Mixer - small hand held appliance with two removable beaters.

Extract, Almond - the extraction of essential almond oil from the nut with alcohol. Found in the baking section of most grocers. We prefer "pure" versions of all extracts. Almond extract can be substituted for vanilla extract in most recipes. Extracts should be stored in a cool, dark pantry.

Extract, Peppermint - the extraction of essential peppermint oil from the mint with alcohol. Found in the baking section of most grocers. We prefer "pure" versions of all extracts. Can be substituted anytime you see Creme de Menthe or Peppermint Schnapps in recipes. Substitute peppermint extract for peppermint oil at 4 to 1 respectively. Extracts should be stored in a cool, dark pantry.

Extract, Vanilla - the extraction of essential vanilla oil from the bean with alcohol. Found in the baking section of most grocers. We prefer "pure" versions of all extracts. Extracts should be stored in a cool, dark pantry.

Flank Steak/Flat Iron (London Broil/Skirt Steak) - slightly different flank cuts of beef. Flank and Skirt Steaks are reasonably priced, flavorful cuts of meat. They are generally packaged folded or rolled because they are thin, long slices of meat. Freeze to extend shelf life.

Flour Tortillas (8" or Fajita Size) - unleavened flat bread made of wheat flour. Keep in refrigerator or freeze to extend shelf life. To soften, microwave for 15 to 30 seconds.

Flour, All-Purpose - a blended wheat flour with an average gluten level. It is available in whole wheat which can be substituted for any recipe, although it will definitely change the taste and texture of your recipe. Try mixing half and half All-Purpose White and Wheat flour together to avoid texture issues. We prefer Unbleached. Store in an air-tight container in your refrigerator.

Here are some quick guides when substituting for other flours.
> 1 Cup Cake Flour = 1 C - 2 T All-Purpose
> 1 Cup Self Rising Flour = 1 C All-Purpose + 1 1/2 t Baking Soda + 1/2 t Salt
> 1 Cup Pastry Flour = 1 C - 1 T All-Purpose

Food Coloring - dyes for food and drink and most readily available in packages of red, yellow, green, and blue. Found in baking section of most grocers.

Fry Pan - (Frying Pan or Skillet) a handled pan used for frying and sauteing. Can be made from non-stick surfaces, stainless steel, and cast iron. We prefer to have lid options for all our pots and pans.

Garlic - a bulb made up of cloves, related to the onion family. Garlic is found in a fresh produce section in large bulbs. A clove is one section of the bulb. Store in a cool dry pantry. To extend the shelf life, freeze the entire bulb. Garlic cloves that are still good should feel firm and have a fresh, garlic smell.
> Substitute 1 Garlic clove for every 1/4 teaspoon Garlic Powder.

Garlic Powder - dehydrated garlic cloves ground into a powder. To retain good flavor and potency, it is best to use dried spices within one year.
> Substitute 1/4 teaspoon Garlic Powder for every Garlic clove.

Ginger (jar or tube) - a processed, vibrant flavored root. Prepared ginger is widely available in a tube or jar. We prefer the tube because of its ease of use and limited added ingredients. Keep tubes and jars in refrigerator. They can be kept in freezer to extend shelf life.

Green Beans (frozen) - podded vegetables found in the frozen food section of most grocers. See package for cooking directions.

Green Onion - (Spring Onions or Scallions) - an onion with long, green stalks and a miniature white bulb. Both the green and white parts of the green onion are edible, although the green stalks are much milder. A good pair of kitchen shears are a quick and easy way to slice them. Green onions should be kept in the refrigerator, sealed in a plastic bag, although it is best to first remove any wilted stalks and to wrap them in a dry paper towel.

Grill Seasonings - a dried spice blend generally made with garlic, onion, salt, pepper, and spices. Found in spice section of most grocers or at meat markets. To retain good flavor and potency, it is best to use dried spices within one year.

Ground Beef/Ground Turkey - beef or turkey which is ground and packaged. Ground beef can be made from different cuts and qualities of meat. They are listed below from highest to lowest fat content.

1. Ground Hamburger
2. Ground Beef
3. Ground Chuck
4. Ground Round
5. Ground Sirloin
6. Lean Ground Beef
7. Extra-Lean Ground Beef

Ground turkey or ground chicken can be substituted for any of the "Stocked" recipes using ground beef. Keep meat in freezer to extend shelf life.

Ground Breakfast Sausage - breakfast sausage without a casing. Found in the meat section of most grocers in plastic wrapped tubes. Experiment with other bulk sausages if you like, including Italian sausage. Keep in freezer to extend shelf life.

Ham (slice or whole) - a thigh cut of pork most often smoked. Turkey ham is an acceptable substitution. Keep in freezer to extend shelf life.

Herbes de Provence - a dried spice blend generally made with rosemary, marjoram, basil, bay leaf, thyme, and lavender. Found in the spice section of most grocers, Herbes de Provence is a unique spice blend with a Mediterranean flavor. To retain good flavor and potency it is best to use dried spices within one year.

Honey - sweet, thick, sugary liquid made from honey bees. Honey is found near jams and jellies in most grocers. It is a natural sweetener and an outstanding anti-oxidant. It can be substituted anytime you see corn syrup with a 1 to 1 ratio, although it may add just a bit more sweetness. Make sure to keep away from children under a year. Store in pantry.

Horseradish, prepared - (Fresh Ground Horseradish) grated root of the horseradish root mixed with vinegar. Keep refrigerated. Prepared horseradish is found, generally, in the refrigerated section near cream cheeses or near other condiments such as barbecue and steak sauces.

Italian Seasonings - a dried spice blend generally made with basil, marjoram, oregano, and sage. Found in the spice section of most grocers. To retain good flavor and potency, it is best to use dried spices within one year.

Jelly Roll Pan - a cookie sheet with short (1") sides.

Ketchup - (Catsup) a sweet and tangy condiment made from tomatoes, sugar, vinegar, and spices. Ketchup is such a basic ingredient and so useful in and of itself that we sometimes forget about its versatility. See the index for lots of recipes using ketchup. Also, try it on your copper pots and pans as a cleaner. The acidity of the tomatoes lifts off the tarnish. Store in the refrigerator after opening. Should last up to a year in the refrigerator.

Lemon Juice - bottled juice of the lemon. Three tablespoons of lemon juice equals about one medium lemon, juiced. Store in refrigerator to extend shelf life.

Lemons - tart yellow citrus fruit. Keep in refrigerator fruit drawer.

Lettuce, Head or Mixed Greens - tender leafy green vegetables. Lettuce comes in many varieties. We love the pre-washed organic mixes that are available at most markets. They are ready to use and have a great combination of healthy greens. We prefer darker greens to iceberg for nutritional purposes; however, its best to use a head of iceberg or bib lettuce when making lettuce wraps. Keep refrigerated.

Limes or Lime Juice - tart green citrus fruit and/or its bottled juice. Keep refrigerated.

Mandarin Oranges (can) - small citrus sections canned in either light syrup or pear juice. We prefer the kind that are canned in pear juice to save on lots of added sugar. To substitute orange juice in recipes, use equal volumes of blended mandarin oranges with the juice.

Maple Syrup - pure maple syrup is produced from the sap of maple trees. The darker the syrup, the more intense the flavor. Grade A Light Amber, Grade A Medium Amber, Grade A Dark Amber, and Grade B define the syrups' color intensity from lightest to darkest. We prefer pure maple syrup for all different kinds of recipes. Refrigerate maple syrup after opening.

Mayonnaise - a condiment made from, oil, egg yolks, lemon juice or vinegar, and seasonings. Reduced fat or light mayonnaise are acceptable substitutions. Refrigerate after opening.

Milk - generally considered cow's milk. Although we usually use skim or low-fat cow's milk, plain soy and rice milk are acceptable alternatives for any of our recipes. Keep refrigerated.

Mini Muffin Pan - a metal pan with 24 small cups that are 1 3/8" diameter and 1" tall sides. We prefer the non-stick variety.

Muffin Pan - a metal pan with 12 cups that are 2 1/2" diameter. It is better to have 2 pans in your inventory and we prefer the non-stick variety.

Mushrooms (can) - mushrooms canned with water and salt. Varieties include whole, sliced, and "pieces and stems." All are suitable for our recipes. We prefer to buy the sliced mushrooms to save us a step. Fresh mushroom can be used as a substitution in any of our recipes, although you should use about 4 times the canned mushroom amount.

Mustard, Dijon - mustard made from brown or black mustard seeds, white wine, vinegar, and spices. Dijon mustard was created by Jean Naigen in Dijon, France in 1856 when he used the juice of unripe grapes instead of vinegar to make a smoother tasting mustard. Refrigerate after opening.

Mustard, Yellow - (Prepared Mustard) is made from white or yellow mustard seeds, water, vinegar, and spices. Yellow mustard can be substituted for ground mustard. Use 1 tablespoon of yellow mustard for every teaspoon of ground mustard. Refrigerate after opening.

Non-Stick Spray - aerosol spray used for creating a non-stick layer on pots and pans to prevent food from adhering to them. It is found in the baking section of most grocers, near the oils. Non-stick spray can be used on most kitchen tool surfaces including pots, pans, spatulas, and mixing bowls.

Nutmeg (whole or ground) - nutmeg is derived from the seed of a plant found in the South Pacific. We prefer using whole nutmeg and grating it fresh with a zester; however, it is available already ground in the spices section of your grocer. To retain good flavor and potency it is best to use dried spices within one year.

Nuts, Almonds - seed of the fruit of the almond tree. Almonds are available raw or roasted and can be found whole, slivered or sliced. Buying slivered or sliced is very convenient. Because of their high fat content, they will become rancid. It is best to store almonds in the refrigerator or freezer in an air-tight container.

Nuts, Peanuts - a shelled legume. Basic peanuts are available in dry roasted, cocktail, and spanish varieties. Peanuts are great in desserts, in Asian dishes, in trail mixes, or by themselves. Don't forget G.O.R.P. - "Good Old Raisins and Peanuts" as a great snack!

Nuts, Pecans - the hard-shelled nut of the pecan or hickory tree. Shelled pecans are available halved, chopped and as chips. Generally "chopped" and "chips" are less expensive. Store in refrigerator or freezer to extend shelf life.

Oil, Extra Virgin Olive - oil extracted from pressing tree ripened olives. "Virgin" refers to hand pressing the olives without any chemical treatment. "Extra Virgin" refers to olives which are cold pressed which makes oil low in acidity and full of fruity flavor. It is great for sautéing but has a lower smoking point, so it is not the best choice for high heat cooking. Keep in a cool dry place.

Oil, Vegetable - oil extracted from vegetables including soy beans, cottonseeds, peanuts, safflower seeds, rape seeds (for canola oil), and sunflower seeds. Refined oils like corn, safflower, canola, and peanut oil have higher smoking points and are better for frying and stir-frying. We like safflower, sunflower, and canola oils for overall cooking and baking. Keep in a cool dry place.

Olives, Black (can) - black fruit from the Olive Tree. American Black olives are not allowed to ferment before being packed which provides a milder flavor. We like to buy these already sliced. Olives add a lot of flavor and act as a great garnish on many dishes. Found in the canned vegetable aisle of most grocers.

Olives, Green or Calamata (jar) -Although Green Olives and Calamata olives are completely different, we provide the option of using either in our recipes. Depending on your personal preference, the recipes will most likely taste differently, but what both do provide is a vibrant, briny taste that is unique. Found in the canned vegetable aisle of most grocers.

> Green Olives - fermented green fruit from the Olive Tree packed in brine.
> Calamata (Greek) Olives - a dark eggplant colored olive with a salty, fruity flavor and meaty texture. Generally packed in vinegar.

Onions, dried minced - (Onion Flakes) dehydrated minced onion. Dried onion is a convenient way to get onions into moist foods. To retain good flavor and potency, it is best to use dried spices within one year.

    1 small onion = 1 t onion powder = 1 T dried minced onion.

Pancake Mix - a prepackaged mix generally made from flour, sugar, powdered milk, and leavening. We choose not to buy the "complete" mixes which allows us to substitute Pancake Mix recipes that call for Baking Mix. Pancake Mix, however, is much easier to find with organic whole wheat flour and without shortening. Keep in a cool, dark pantry.

Parchment Paper - a baking paper infused with silicone to create non-stick surfaces. We love to also use it to "quick-thaw" our Frozen Bread Dough and to bake chicken. Found either in paper products of most grocers or by cooking and baking supplies.

Pasta, Penne, Fusilli, Gemili or Farfalle - dried, shaped pasta made from, in its most simple form, a flour and water mixture. We basically want you to have short pasta in your pantry. These shorter, wider shapes can stand up to heavier sauces and provide interest to the dish. The shape choice is up to you, but we suggest:

    Penne: Little tubes
    Fusilli: Twists
    Gemili: Two pasta lengths twisted together
    Farfalle: Bowties

Pasta, Thin - dried, thin, long pasta made from, in its most simple form, a flour and water mixture. Again, the specific style is up to you. We don't recommend using Angel Hair because it is so fine it can't stand up to all sauces. These are our suggestions from thinnest to thickest:

1) Thin Spaghetti
2) Spaghetti
3) Linguine Fine

4) Linguine
5) Fettuccine

Peanut Butter, creamy - paste made from ground peanuts and often combined with oil and sugar. We prefer creamy peanut butter because of its versatility. Peanut Butter can generally be stored in the pantry unless it is all natural or organic. If that is the case, open it, stir in all the oil that has settled at the top, and then refrigerate.

Pears (can) - canned, subtly sweet, and fragrant fruit. Available in "halves" or "sliced." We prefer to buy pears in 100% juice although they are also available in heavy or light syrup.

Peas (frozen) - a podded fruit removed from pod and frozen. Found in the frozen food section, peas are wonderful in recipes or as a quick salad topping. Just thaw peas and drain, and they are ready to go!

Pepper, Ground / Peppercorns - fermented and dried berries of an evergreen vine. Different colors of peppercorns depend on when the fruit is plucked. We prefer to use whole peppercorns and freshly grind at the table or into recipes. Found in the spice section of most grocers. To retain good flavor and potency, it is best to use dried spices within one year.

Pine Nuts - (Pignoli) are soft, sweet, buttery seeds of pine trees. Pine nuts are generally found in the fresh produce section of most grocers. They can be used in both savory dishes and sweet desserts. Keep in a plastic container in refrigerator for up to a month or in your freezer for up to three months. Pistachios make a good substitution in most dishes.

Pineapple, slices or chunks (can) - a canned, very juicy fruit with a tangy sweet taste. Available in "rings," "chunks," and "crushed." For all recipes we prefer "rings" or "chunks." We prefer to buy pineapple in 100% juice although it is also available in heavy or light syrup.

Pita Bread - flat bread made with a pocket. Found near the deli counter of most grocers. Can be frozen to extend shelf life.

Plastic Wrap - (Cling Wrap) a plastic film used for wrapping and preserving food. Most often it is made from PVC; however, there are now non-PVC-alternatives available at larger grocers and health food stores. Found near the paper products of most grocers.

Potatoes (Russet, Sweet, or Yukon Gold) (fresh) - starchy, tuberous, root vegetables. Store potatoes in a cool and well ventilated place for, 2 to 4 months. Do not refrigerate or freeze raw potatoes because their starch will turn into sugar.

> Russet: A great all purpose potato for mashed, baked, escalloped and french fried potatoes. If potatoes have a lot of large "eyes," do not buy them.

> Sweet Potatoes: a very healthy option to substitute for white potatoes. They have orange flesh and a high natural sugar content.

> Yukon Gold Potatoes: yellow, thin fleshed potatoes have a rich creamy flavor.

Poultry Seasonings - a dried spice blend generally made with sage, thyme, pepper, marjoram, and sometimes cloves. Found in the spice section of most grocers. To retain good flavor and potency, it is best to use dried spices within one year.

Puff Pastry Sheets (frozen) - a light and flaky, unleavened pastry sheet made, generally, from flour, butter, salt, and cold water. Found in the frozen food section of most grocers near frozen pie crusts. We prefer to buy it in sheets which adds to its versatility. Make sure dough is chilled before baking to ensure that pastry puffs as much as possible.

Pumpkin Pie Spice - a dried spice blend generally made with cinnamon, ginger, nutmeg, and cloves. To retain good flavor and potency, it is best to use dried spices within one year.

Raisins - dried red or yellow grapes. Available dark plum, black, and golden varieties. Choose based on personal preference. Because drying is a natural preservation method, raisins, in an airtight container, stay fresh a long time. Toss if they begin to get really hard or crystalize.

Ranch / Buttermilk Dressing - generally made with vegetable oil, buttermilk, water, sugar, garlic, onion, salt, and spices. Our only purchased salad dressing; this dressing can be used on salads, as a condiment on sandwiches, and also mixes wonderfully with salsa, tabasco, barbecue sauce, and tomato paste for dips and dressings. Refrigerate after opening.

Raspberry Jam/Jelly - Jam is made by boiling fruit and includes pieces of the fruit. Jelly is made from fruit juice and does not have any fruit parts in it. Try to buy "seedless" which blends easier and is void of those pesky little seeds. Refrigerate after opening.

Red Pepper Flakes - dried and crushed red chili peppers. We love red pepper flakes for providing a heat to dishes without the addition of vinegar. Generally, the longer the pepper flakes cook or stand, the hotter the dish becomes. To retain good flavor and potency, it is best to use dried spices within one year.

Relish, Sweet or Dill - finely chopped, pickled cucumbers. Strictly a personal preference. Depending on which you decide, the recipes in this book will vary significantly in taste, but will still work great in their own way. Store in the refrigerator after opening. Found near pickles and olives in most grocers.
  Sweet - generally made with sugar, vinegar, water, and salt
  Dill - generally made with vinegar, water, dill weed, and garlic.

Rice, Jasmine and/or Brown - grains from marshy grasses. We use these rices interchangeably in all recipes, although brown rice tends to give food a crunchier texture and may require a longer cooking time.
  Jasmine - long grained, fragrant, Thai rice. Basmati can be substituted.
  Brown Rice - healthy rice grains which retain the natural bran layer.

Roasted Red Peppers (jar) - sweet red peppers fire roasted and then packed in water or vinegar. Roasted Red Peppers are usually found in the international section of most grocers, but they might also be by canned/jarred vegetables. The peppers are often packed in water or vinegar, so buy according to taste preference although those packed in vinegar will last longer after they are opened. Refrigerate after opening.

Salsa - "Salsa" is Spanish for "sauce." Commonly known as a condiment made from chopped vegetables and seasonings. Salsa is generally found in the international section of most grocers; however, some fresh varieties are also found in the fresh produce section. Refrigerate after opening.

Salt - mined sodium chloride. Salt is the most necessary and basic of all seasonings and is available to buy in many different forms. We feel that table salt is the most versatile. Found in the spice section of most grocers.

Saucepan - a two or three quart, long handled pot. We prefer to have lid options for all our pots and pans.

Skewers, Wooden - skewers made often from bamboo. We love to keep these around for shish-kebabs. Make sure to soak them in water before grilling to keep them from igniting. Found in the housewares or kitchen gadget sections of most grocers.

Shallot/Onion - skinned bulb vegetables. Shallots taste like a combination of onions and garlic with a mild and rich flavor. Do not buy shallots if they have already begun to sprout. If you would prefer to use onions, it's better to choose Yellow or Vidalia onions which tend to have a milder taste. Any "Stocked" recipe can use either shallots or onions. In general you use half the amount of shallots compared to onions. Shallots should be kept in a cool, dark pantry much like garlic. Store onions in a cool, dark pantry. Do not freeze.

Shrimp, raw, peeled and de-veined (frozen) - crustacean shellfish. We buy uncooked Shrimp for their versatility. We also prefer to buy the Shrimp peeled and de-veined to ease tremendously in their preparation.

300

Sour Cream or Plain Yogurt - We like having the choice of using either sour cream or plain yogurt interchangeably. Although the tastes may be slightly different, we allow your personal preference to dictate your choice. If using as a condiment on tacos or burritos, we suggest using sour cream. They are both found in the refrigerated dairy section of most grocers.

> Sour Cream is a cultured cream which is allowed to sour.
>
> Yogurt is bacterial fermented milk.

Soy Sauce - (Soya Sauce) is a fermented sauce made from soybeans, roasted grain, water, and salt. Low-Sodium versions are completely acceptable to use for all recipes. We use Soy Sauce as a seasoning at the dinner table for rice and vegetables. Found in the Asian area of the international section of most grocers.

Spinach (bag) (frozen) - dark green leafy vegetable found in the frozen foods section of most grocers. We much prefer to buy it "chopped" and in a bag instead of the box, so we only have to thaw what we need. See package for cooking directions. Great in soups, stews, dips, and pastas.

Stock Pot - six or more quart, large pot with small handles on two sides. We prefer to have lid options for all our pots and pans.

Springform Pan - metal baking pan which sides can be unhinged and removed from the bottom once the dish is completed.

Storage Bags, Resealable Gallon - bags made from thin, flexible, plastic film with a zippered top to allow it to be repeatedly opened and closed. We love to use these bags to marinades our meats. Found near the paper product section of most grocers.

Sugar, Brown - white sugar combined with molasses. The darker the sugar the higher the content of molasses. Brown sugar can be used as a sweetener on cereals, fruits, and in beverages. It is also good to have it around for baking because of its added flavor and moisture content. Keeping a slice of bread in your air-tight container of brown sugar can aid in keeping it soft. Found in the baking section of most grocers.

Sugar, Granulated - white sugar granules from highly refined beet or cane sugar. The basic sugar in your cupboard. Found in the baking section of most grocers.

Sugar, Powdered - (Confectioner's or Icing Sugar) a finely ground form of highly refined beet or cane sugar generally mixed with corn starch. Great as a dusting for cakes and brownies. Also used in frostings, candies, and icings. Found in the baking section of most grocers.

Tabasco/Hot Sauce - generally made from hot peppers, vinegar, and salt and then aged. Tabasco sauce is generally found by the ketchup and mustards at most grocers. Tabasco can be substituted for cayenne pepper although Tabasco will add a vinegar taste to the dish. The substitution should be for every 1/4 t of cayenne pepper, substitute 6 - 8 drops. The flavor stays better in the refrigerator. If it changes to a dark color, it is probably best to toss it.

Toothpicks - a small stick, usually made from wood, with pointed ends. We prefer the non-colored toothpicks to avoid color running into our food. Found in the paper products or kitchen gadget section of most grocers.

Tomato Paste (can or tube) - made from tomatoes whose skins and seeds have been removed. They are cooked and pureed until a thick paste has formed. Tomato paste provides richness to sauces, soups, and chilies. Although it is sometimes hard to find, we love the paste in a tube because we waste less. Refrigerate after opening.

Tomato Sauce (can) - a puree of tomatoes. Tomato sauce is a wonderful, easy way to make tomato based sauces, soups, stews, and chilies.

Tomatoes (fresh) - soft, often red, fruit. It is best to store tomatoes on a countertop, out of the refrigerator to prevent them from becoming mealy. There are many varieties of fresh tomatoes, but we generally choose:

   Beefsteak - large, sweet and juicy, used for sauces and great sliced for sandwiches or cut up for salads.

   Roma - oval or pear shaped tomato known for having less juice and seeds. Great for dips and salsas.

   For every 1 1/2 cups of chopped fresh tomatoes, you can substitute one drained 15 oz. can of diced tomatoes.

Tomatoes Diced (can) - tomatoes that have been diced and packed in water and salt. Found in most grocers canned tomato section. We love the ease and versatility of diced tomatoes.

   One drained can of diced tomatoes can generally be substituted for every 1 1/2 cups of chopped fresh tomatoes.

Tortilla Chips - baked or fried chips made from corn or flour tortillas. Tortilla chips are available in may shapes and sizes. They are also available in flour, yellow, or blue corn. Found in the salty snack section of most grocers.

Vanilla Ice Cream - frozen dessert made, generally, from milk, cream, sugar, and vanilla. Low fat and low sugar versions are acceptable substitutions.

Vinegar, Aged Balsamic - oxidation of the unfermented juice of a grape, aged in wooden barrels. Look for vinegar that is from Modena, a region of Italy. The longer the vinegar has been allowed to age, the sweeter the flavor. Balsamic vinegar can be used in dressings and savory sauces and is sweet enough to pour over fruit as a dessert. Found near salad dressings in most grocers.

Vinegar, Red Wine - oxidation of the alcohol in red wine. A very basic vinegar great in dressings and marinades. Found near salad dressings in most grocers.

Vinegar, White Wine - oxidation of the alcohol in white wine. Used in salad dressings and many other recipes. Use as a substitution for rice wine vinegar and cider vinegar. Found near salad dressings in most grocers.

Worcestershire Sauce - a sauce made up of aged vinegars, tamarind, anchovies, spices, and sugars. This sauce has a rich and savory sauce. Anytime a recipe calls for fish sauce you can substitute it with half worcestershire sauce and half soy sauce. Found near condiments like steak sauce in most grocers.

304

Ingredient Index

C

D

Recipe Index

Acknowledgments

The Stocked Kitchen™ would not be possible without the support and help of so many people. We are very thankful for all of you who have believed in this concept and extended, willingly, your time, talent, and love.

SPECIAL THANKS TO:

Sue Beecham. We are forever grateful for your photos, kindness, and friendship. You are so very talented and fun to work with. We will always fondly remember taste testing cold "photo session" food with you and Jason.

SUE BEECHAM PHOTOGRAPHY, LLC

WWW.SUEBEECHAMPHOTO.COM

Kristin Schutte. Neither of us are English majors, so we will always appreciate your time and knowledge of the English language. Thank you so much for your help in making this book "correct."

Andrea Alfano. Thank you so much for your willingness to help, particularly with recipe testing and product marketing. You are lovely and a joy.

CSP, Inc. Thanks to all who have worked hard to make our dream a reality!

www.csp-inc.com

Kelly Larson from Sweet Temptations, Grand Haven, Michigan. Thank you for all your ideas and allowing us to taste test!

Christi, Dawn, and Karen, our original testers. Thank you so much for your friendship, enthusiasm, and great ideas!

FROM SARAH

To my children, who are the greatest happiness of my life, thank you both for your patience and love. To my parents, Sue and Norb, I am so thankful for all of your love, support, and hard work. This book would not exist without you. Mom and Grandma, thank you for teaching me that love is the most important ingredient in great cooking. To my brother, Pete, thank you for your support, guidance and love. To Christi and Megan who, no matter how much time passes, are always there for me. Thank you for your input and encouragement. To my wonderful In-Law Family, for your enthusiasm and support. And to the love of my life, Larry, you are the best person I have ever known. I am thankful, everyday, for you and the life we have created together.

FROM STACEY

I live every day for my children and hope that I might inspire them. Thank you to Andrew and Charlie for teaching me, just as much as I teach you. To my parents and sisters, thank you all for your love and support as I chase my dream. To my best friend Karen, thank you for all your love, encouragement, and honesty. Our friendship is unwavering, and I am grateful for that. To my husband, Craig, thank you for believing in me and inspiring me to be a better person. I am always in awe of your patience and kindness, and I look forward to growing old together. I love you.

Lastly, to all the mothers before us who invented a better way to do something, you are our inspiration.

NOTES

NOTES

The Stocked Heart™ ♡

Statistically, someone who picks up this book will be affected or know someone affected by the issues below. There are solutions and people who want to help. Please contact these organizations if you or anyone you know is in need of their services.

National Domestic Violence Hotline
1-800-799-SAFE   or   1-866-331-8453 TTY
www.ndvh.org

If you or someone you know is in an abusive relationship, please call. Hotline advocates are available for victims and anyone calling on their behalf to provide crisis intervention, safety planning, information, and referrals to agencies in all 50 states, Puerto Rico, and the U.S. Virgin Islands. Assistance is available in English and Spanish and 170 other languages. Safety Alert: Computer use can be monitored and is impossible to completely clear. If you are afraid your internet and/or computer usage might be monitored, please use a safer computer and/or call the Hotline or Helpline. Advocates are available 24 hours a day, 365 days a year.

Postpartum Support International
1-800-944-4PPD
www.postpartum.net

If you or someone you know might be experiencing symptoms of prenatal or postpartum mood or anxiety disorder, know that it is treatable. There are PSI Coordinators throughout the world who provide information and support. There is someone in your area who can help you if you are experiencing any of the following: depression, irritability, exhaustion, feeling unlike yourself, sadness, anger, guilt, worry, or feelings of inadequacy.